COACHING
for
RESULTS

The 5 *TIPS that Drive Performance*

Steven J. Stowell, Ph.D.
Cherissa S. Newton, M.ED
Eric D. Mead

CMOE Press
Salt Lake City, Utah

CMOE, Inc.
9146 South 700 East
Sandy, UT 84070

ISBN-13: 978-1-942269-02-1
Library of Congress Control Number: 2019937887

First Edition
Printed in the USA
Text Editing: Emily Hodgson-Soule
Cover Design: Design Type Service
Typesetting: Design Type Service

This book and other CMOE Press publications are available on Amazon.com, BarnesandNoble.com, and by ordering directly from the publisher.

CMOE Press
+1 801 569 3444
www.CMOE.com

Acknowledgements

We want to offer our sincere thanks to everyone who assisted us throughout this lengthy writing journey. Compiling years of research, experience, and observation into a third book on the topic of coaching was a challenge that we were only able to take on because of the valuable roles that others played in our inspiration—and their patience as we made this book a reality.

Although each person who has touched this book has played an invaluable part in bringing it to life, there are a few specific people who have helped *Coaching for Results: The 5 TIPS that Drive Performance* reach its full potential. We'd like to take this opportunity to show them our gratitude here:

- Stephanie Mead, MBA; Emily Hodgson-Soule, MPC; and Kelsi Mackay, Senior CMOE Account Manager for their creative minds and their willingness to help complete the book.
- The CMOE facilitators and team who shared their ideas and the insights they have gained over the years they've spent delivering the Coaching TIPS2™ Workshop to our valued clients.
- Our families who, as always, were so supportive during this process.

Thank you!

Table of Contents

CHAPTER
1

Coaching – What it is and Why it's Needed

"In spite of unseasonable wind, snow and unexpected weather of all sorts, a gardener still plants. And tends what they have planted...believing that spring will come."

—**Mary Anne Radmacher**

If you ask a group of people the simple question, "What is coaching?" you will likely hear a variety of definitions. Over the years, the term "coaching" has been used in many contexts. In the 1500s, the term "coach" referred to the horse-drawn carriage that served as a means of transportation. In the 1800s, the term was used to refer to the tutoring process and to the training of athletes. In the 1900s, it became the job title for the leader of a team participating in sports. More recently, however, people in many types of organizations have completely adopted this term to refer both to effective leadership and feedback and to mutually beneficial relationships.

Coaching is a process. It consists of the actions or skills used by a leader or individual that bring about the desired end result. At its most basic level, coaching represents a way to communicate openly, clearly, and candidly about important matters. At a deeper level, coaching is about sharing honest feedback, communicating expectations, identifying performance-improvement opportunities, encouraging development and growth, and assisting with action-planning and execution of the desired change. We want to emphasize that coaching is not a process simply designed to "fix" problems, although coaches can frequently turn a problem, issue, or mistake into a great teaching moment. Coaching also includes helping people grow, change, and improve. It is interesting to note that the root meaning of "to coach" is based on the idea of bringing a person from where he or she is to the point where he or she wants or needs to be. Albert Einstein, while remembered as a genius, began to talk very late into childhood. At the dinner table one night, Einstein broke his silence by saying, *"The soup is too hot."* His parents later asked why he had never before said a word, to which Einstein replied, *"Because up to now, everything was in order."* While this story about a beloved, eccentric historical figure is quite funny, this is often how managers and leaders approach coaching: they don't speak up until something is blatantly wrong or desperately needed. Our focus with coaching is aimed at consistently influencing and developing the employees' skills, motivation, attitude, judgment, or ability to perform, as well as their willingness to contribute to the organization's goals. You simply can't grow a successful organization if leaders don't talk with people openly about their performance and contribution to the business.

Unfortunately, coaching skills are typically rated very low in organization and leadership assessments, indicating a need for

improvement. In fact, a study conducted by the Association for Talent Development found that only 27% of organizations incorporate coaching into their talent development portfolios, yet 69% of learning and business leaders "felt that coaching contributes highly to improved communication" and almost the same percentage believe that "coaching is a major driver of gains in each of the following areas: employee engagement, the transfer of learning skills to on-the-job performance and productivity" (TD Magazine, December 2014). Furthermore, Gallup research (May 2017) indicates that "about one in four employees 'strongly agree' that their manager provides meaningful feedback to them—or that the feedback they receive helps them do better at work." This is certainly compelling, but what is really concerning is that only "21% of employees 'strongly agree' that their performance is managed in a way that motivates them to do outstanding work." So how do we get the most out of the modern workforce? We give them what they want and need: high-quality coaching and feedback.

"Coach" is Not Just A Title

Many organizations use the title "coach" to refer to leaders of departments or teams. However, just because they use this title doesn't mean that these people are coaching their direct reports and co-workers, or even that they know how to do it! When we use the terms "coach" and "coaching" throughout this book, we are referring to something you *do*. It is a responsibility, a task, and a process that leads to better behaviors and results for both the coach as well as the person on the receiving end of the coaching. Because of this, it is not a title or responsibility to be taken lightly. While in this book we often refer to or use examples of a leader /team-member relationship, we want to emphasize that the coaching process is for anyone who might want to exercise positive influence and help others succeed. It starts with the ability to communicate to a higher level. It is a proven mechanism for unleashing the performance of others and building the talents of the people who will take on the future. We don't feel that being an excellent coach is a genetic gift given to a select few people. To the contrary, we believe that coaching embodies a unique set of abilities, personal values, and inner characteristics that can be learned and developed with time and dedication. It's also important to remember that not all coaches are the same, nor do they coach in the same way. While we will recommend a process to follow when coaching, each coach's ability and style will be different and will vary even further when the coaching approach is adapted to the specific needs of the person being coached.

The perspective a person has on a situation makes a huge impact on its possible outcomes. Here is a story to illustrate our point: Many years ago, two salesmen were sent to Africa by a British shoe manufacturer to investigate and report back on market potential. The first salesman reported back, "There is no potential here—nobody wears shoes." The second salesman reported back, "There is massive potential here—nobody wears shoes." The takeaway is this: while one person might think that coaching isn't needed within their team or organization, another could be thinking about the countless opportunities that could be gained from coaching. Most organizations in today's demand-filled business environment have found that finding, engaging, and then retaining talent is critical to their success. That alone provides many coaching opportunities. Leaders must capitalize on any chance they get to engage the hearts and minds of team members and help them reach their full potential, setting the organization up for sustained growth and prosperity, achievement, or gain.

Before jumping into the process itself, let's lay the groundwork by sharing our thoughts in response to the questions we get asked most often.

Who Should I Coach?

A common misconception is that coaching should focus on the most challenging employees, those who require a lot of time and attention from leaders. The old saying, "The squeaky wheel gets the grease" illustrates this concept perfectly. However, the true purpose of coaching should be to address the behaviors and opportunities of good or competent performers. In a common work setting, "competent" performers make up a big portion of an organization's talent—as much as 80%. Coaches can make the greatest difference by attending to this larger group of people and working towards unlocking *their* potential, rather than focusing a disproportionate amount of their time and attention on top performers and underperformers.

Unfortunately, many leaders misunderstand or avoid the responsibility of coaching others, despite the fact that the process can be extremely rewarding for all parties. Coaching enables others to grow and learn from the experiences, activities, and journeys that we share with them. Ultimately, the coaching investment leads to positive action, new skills, and performance results that are critical to the coachees' long-term success, as well as that of the organization. In our executive-coaching work, we find that leaders typically don't fail because of poor technical skills but due to their inability to work with others, to communicate effectively, and to inspire people. While a focus on bottom-line targets and results is critical, leaders cannot overlook the fact that results are best achieved through developing others to reach those goals.

Coaching is certainly an essential *leadership* skill, but it's also useful for the other members of an organization, regardless of their rank or title. Coaching isn't just a skill to be used in a "top-down" way by management alone! Coaching skills can also be used by team members to share feedback and ideas to improve workplace performance with their leaders. Team members should also coach their peers to enhance cooperation and collaboration throughout the organization. For organizations to establish a coaching culture, everyone has to be willing to coach and be coached, including leaders and peers. Consider the following story: A man stood at the corner of a busy intersection, waiting to cross the road. This man was visually impaired and was hopeful that someone else would soon need to cross the road so he could have someone guide him. Just then, another man appeared, and while he was waiting for the traffic to appear the first man said, "Excuse me. I'm blind and was wondering if you would mind guiding me across the road." Unbeknownst to the first man, the second man was blind as well. Without saying a word, he took the arm of the man and together they both crossed the road. The second visually impaired man was the jazz pianist George Shearing. He is quoted in Bartlett's Anecdotes as saying after the event, "What could I do? I took him across and it was the biggest thrill of my life."

In some situations, individuals, teams, and organizations may feel like they're blindly moving forward or like the blind

Team members should coach their peers to enhance cooperation and collaboration.

are leading the blind. Yet in these challenging situations, there is great power when people utilize the talents they have, come together, and collaborate on solutions to the tough challenges and obstacles that lie in the path of achieving goals and strategies. What it takes is people who are willing to coach each other and developing a culture where people take on the risks and challenges together. These opportunities to synergize and collaborate can become the biggest thrills of our professional lives and do tremendous good for organizations.

When Do I Coach?

We have identified two main types of coaching situations: formal and informal. Formal coaching discussions are deliberate and planned in advance. Some examples of formal coaching situations are quarterly performance reviews, project reviews, or career- and development-planning conversations. Informal coaching is "on the move" or "in the moment" and happens during unplanned and spontaneous events that surface on a day-to-day basis. One example of an informal coaching situation is having a quick conversation in the break room after observing a process breakdown. Other examples include following up on a delegated assignment, a safety concern, quality issues, or opportunities for continuous improvement. Typically, leaders will have far fewer occasions for formal coaching discussions than informal ones, but both are important in building relationships and engaging human capital. Regardless of how it

> **The true test of a coach is his or her ability to facilitate an open and constructive dialogue about others' success in working toward strategic goals and operational excellence.**

is used, coaching is rarely a one-time event. Instead, coaching is an ongoing process of building partnerships to support an organization's ongoing improvement.

Ideally, you should be regularly engaged in coaching people before a pressing need for coaching arises. If that is not possible, you should hold a coaching conversation immediately after you recognize the need for coaching. If you continually put off and avoid coaching, issues will worsen over time and create even more issues down the line. This can lead to frustration and a breakdown in trust.

How Do I Coach People in a Flexible Way?

Every coaching situation comes with numerous factors that must be taken into consideration in order for the coaching to be successful. Culture is one of those factors. People have different personality styles, backgrounds, values, etc., and everyone prefers to be coached in a different fashion. People in South America and people in North America have different styles and communication preferences. People in Asia have different requirements and expectations than people in Europe. Another factor is the style and needs of the person you are coaching. "High-context" people need a lot of background information and explanation, as well as plenty of time to respond and react. If you are a "low-context" coach, you could make the mistake of rushing through the coaching topic too quickly or coming across as insensitive, domineering, or aggressive. You will need to anticipate needs, think about the personality and style of the individual, and then make any necessary adjustments to how you apply the coaching process under a given set of circumstances. Understanding the factors at play will help you choose the most appropriate approach to the coaching process.

How Do I Make Coaching a Positive Experience?

Being coached doesn't have to be intimidating for the coachee (or the coach). What *should* scare you is what can happen when people don't interact with each other on a regular basis. Coaching should be a positive method of helping others, without one person taking too much control or becoming overly dependent on the other person for answers. In today's fast-paced world, most people operate under pressure. Too many work environments are characterized by negativity, destructive conflict, dejection, backbiting, and inaction. It is not uncommon to feel attacked when people confront us with abrupt or aggressive feedback; too many people are hurt by "friendly fire" when their associates, friends, and leaders inadvertently shoot them down. We need to change that. Organizations need partners who can create a safe environment for honest dialogue where people can be respectful of differences and openly share what they see, think, and feel. Coaches work to promote the talents and potential of the individuals on the team and motivate people to get excited about helping the group achieve its purpose. They set the right tone with their team and infuse their coaching with support, positivity, and openness, even if it is a difficult topic. While coaching isn't the answer to all problems, it does provide a foundation upon which to build the future.

Coaching: What It Is and Isn't

A simple dichotomy can be helpful when trying to better understand the essence of coaching in a business setting:

What It Is	What It Is Not
• A learnable skill	• A quick fix
• Highly effective	• Something that works every time
• A growth process	• An event
• Something that requires patience	• Techniques
• Value-driven	• Common practice
• Practical	• Only "problem-focused"
• Useful for all team members	• A one-time, across-the-board "program"
• A developmental experience	• Automatic
• Builds on strengths	• Reactive
• Both formal and spontaneous	• Control, order, and compliance
• A choice	• Only one-on-one
• Proactive problem-solving	• A Noun: Thing/Object
• Dialogue, collaboration, and learning	• Manipulation
• Useful in a group setting	• One-way
• A Verb: Dynamic/Action	• Top-down

Changing the Coaching Culture

The business-coaching approach started with a "my way or the highway," very directive approach to coaching employees. This obviously doesn't work very effectively, particularly with today's workforce. More recently, we've seen a trend that has moved to the other extreme: an overly soft, time-consuming, question-driven process. This notion is based more on a sports philosophy than a business perspective and is an internally focused process that assumes the person being coached already knows what the issues are and how to improve them. While this approach works for some, it fails to serve the majority of business coaches (or the people they need to coach).

Managers and leaders need a coaching technique that allows them to be declarative when necessary, an approach to performance coaching that encourages candid, open communication and informs people when they are off-track, have development opportunities, or are on track. In business, leaders have to be able to articulate their perspective and expectations without psychological game-playing that can confuse coaches and consume a lot of time. When we coach people, we are attempting to address and explore important topics. An effective coaching conversation is courageous and free of fear and intimidation. Parties share their viewpoints in an atmosphere of trust, reflecting on problems to solve and opportunities to pursue. As ideas are generated, effective communication skills are essential; both parties must be able to listen and learn from each other, achieve understanding, and then collaborate on how to be more effective in the future.

Successful coaching helps the coachee stay focused on a common objective without using fear, threats, pessimism, or other negative tactics.

Coaching requires the coach and coachee to achieve common ground and direction through open and candid dialogue. Effective dialogue between two people can lead to clear direction, mutual agreements, solutions, and creativity. These elements enable people to perform their roles with greater commitment. The coaching process helps people grow and learn—and ultimately live, share, sustain meaningful relationships, and produce better results. But to grow, people most often need straightforward feedback that is given in a supportive way; a constructive coaching conversation that is an honest, forthright assessment of the coachee's strengths and weaknesses. In true coaching relationships, the leader is a partner in helping the coachee identify how to make lasting changes and gain the ability to generate sustained performance and results.

It cannot be denied that when individual contributors receive good coaching from peers and leaders, their performance and value increases. People are important assets for organizations and it is a leader's responsibility to maintain and fully leverage those assets. Coaching is the mechanism for getting the most and best out of your valuable team members. Some coaches find that some or all aspects of coaching others come to them naturally. Others need to learn or fine tune these skills. If that is your need, you've come to the right place. The main objective of this book is to provide you with a practical and proven coaching model that will help you build a positive coaching culture within your organization. Here you will find the fundamental knowledge and skills that everyone who wants to be a better coach must learn. Let's dive into the essential behaviors that will help you become an influential, world-class coach.

Coaching Effectiveness Self-Assessment

If you would like more insight regarding your current coaching strengths and opportunities for improvement, complete the following Coaching Effectiveness Self-Assessment. The ten questions found in the assessment below will help you pinpoint areas to focus on as you learn more about the Coaching TIPS$^{2™}$ Model and process.

How effective are you at the following? (1 = low effectiveness, 10 = high effectiveness)

1.	Listening and allowing coachees to share their thoughts, ideas, and perspective during a coaching discussion	1 2 3 4 5 6 7 8 9 10
2.	Clearly giving credit and recognition to coachees for their contributions and efforts	1 2 3 4 5 6 7 8 9 10
3.	Making the coachee aware of and clearly defining a specific concern or opportunity for coaching	1 2 3 4 5 6 7 8 9 10
4.	Clarifying or defining performance standards or expectations during coaching discussions	1 2 3 4 5 6 7 8 9 10
5.	Helping coachees "step back" and examine their actions, attitudes, skills, or decisions from a different point of view	1 2 3 4 5 6 7 8 9 10
6.	Helping coachees understand how their actions contribute to or detract from the overall success of the team or organization's mission and goals	1 2 3 4 5 6 7 8 9 10
7.	Giving the coachee the opportunity to develop or share ideas for action plans rather than rigidly controlling the solution	1 2 3 4 5 6 7 8 9 10
8.	Clearly asking for a commitment to the action plan and agreements made during a coaching discussion	1 2 3 4 5 6 7 8 9 10
9.	Helping coachees see the potential pay-offs and benefits of a solution or new approach	1 2 3 4 5 6 7 8 9 10
10.	Following up to provide support and reinforcement and ensure accountability for the progress being made on plans and agreements	1 2 3 4 5 6 7 8 9 10

Interpreting Your Score

Items with a score of 5 or below should be considered an opportunity to enhance your coaching skills, while items scored 6 or above are likely a strength or something you do with consistency. As you read on, you will see how the questions in the Self-Assessment align with the Coaching TIPS²™ process. Pay particular attention to the chapters that include ideas on how to improve your personal coaching effectiveness. Even if you don't have any items scored 5 or below, we encourage you to identify at least one area in which your coaching skills could be enhanced.

Question 1: Support (*Chapter 3*)
Question 2: Support (*Chapter 3*)
Question 3: Topic (*Chapter 4*)
Question 4: Topic (*Chapter 4*)
Question 5: Impact (*Chapter 5*)
Question 6: Impact (*Chapter 5*)
Question 7: Plan (*Chapter 6*)
Question 8: Plan (*Chapter 6*)
Question 9: Sustain (*Chapter 7*)
Question 10: Sustain (*Chapter 7*)

Some of these skills may come more naturally to you; you may need to work hard on some others in order for them to become fully developed. Don't be discouraged! You've come to the right place. The ideas we share in this book will help you in your personal development journey. As you build on your strengths and address your opportunities for improvement, remember that developing the skills of a world-class coach comes one step at a time.

2

Introduction to the Coaching TIPS²™ Model

Many leaders find coaching to be one of the most challenging parts of their job because they haven't developed the practical skills or process for doing it effectively. We answered this challenge that leaders in all types of organizations face by developing a simple, five-step coaching process that will guide you through developmental and performance-related coaching discussions of all kinds. Whether you are brand new to coaching or are an experienced coach looking to further solidify your skills, a systematic and proven method for how to coach others is invaluable.

These elements of effective coaching discussions aren't based simply on our opinions or gut instinct. To the contrary, our organization has been conducting ground-breaking research for decades and this research is the foundation for our coaching models and methodology. The Coaching TIPS²™ Model evolved from our first formal study in 1985 which sought to identify the behaviors of world-class coaches. CMOE's original Eight-Step Coaching Model developed out of that research. The Model has continued to be validated and revised through additional applied research and through the consulting and training we do with organizations around the world. The Model mirrors what we've seen and heard in the research and provides people with a framework for establishing quality interactions with others on important topics. Our most recent research indicated that some managers need a more streamlined version of the Model, one they could use to coach people on the spot. These five steps or behaviors encompass what it takes to coach and build partnerships and are reflected in a simple acronym: Coaching TIPS²™. This Model helps coaches quickly and easily recall the essential components of a successful coaching conversation, regardless of the length of the discussion.

This chapter provides a broad overview of the Coaching TIPS²™ Model, giving you a solid understanding of the framework as a whole. A detailed explanation of the individual components of the Model follow in later chapters, allowing you to focus in on specific skills you would like to develop or learn about in greater depth.

The Coaching TIPS²™ Model

The Coaching TIPS²™ Model is neither a prescription nor a "cookbook" of techniques; it's a clear and concise process or framework that coaches can use to guide their coaching discussions in productive ways. One of the Model's strengths is that it provides structure but also allows for significant flexibility—an absolute requirement given the vast array of situations and personalities that a coach will encounter.

We have often likened the Coaching TIPS²™ Model to the keys on a piano; the leaders who use this Model are like composers who use the various notes on the keyboard to create musical pieces of vastly different styles. Some people may simply start playing and compose their music on the fly, while others might prefer to plan and compose the musical score before they even approach the keyboard. Others may use a combination of both approaches: some initial planning combined with a lot of spontaneity as the rhythm and tone evolve and the character of the piece emerges. Like music, there is room for a systematic method as well as creativity and flexibility when applying the Coaching TIPS²™ Model.

For those who are newer to coaching, for whom coaching comes less naturally, and even for the most experienced coaches, the Coaching TIPS²™ Model is a proven, straightforward framework. This Model will allow you to complete the "pre-flight check" before taking off with a coaching discussion. Then, if a person experiences vertigo during the dialogue, the Model becomes a point of reference: something coaches can use to reorient themselves, much like using a map.

The Model is a guide designed to build inclusive relationships, create understanding, share wisdom, and solve challenges through open and constructive interactions. It also helps people achieve constructive openness where they can share their thoughts, discuss contrasting visions, exchange honest feedback, and resolve differences respectfully. The Model is not designed to be a crafty way to lecture to or reprimand the coachee in any form or fashion. It is, however, designed to level the playing field when it comes to engaging in open dialogue. The Coaching TIPS²™ Model helps you and the other party put things into perspective so that minor issues aren't blown out of proportion–and major issues aren't glossed over.

Through careful and thoughtful application, the Model becomes something to actively *practice*, not just advocate;

something that can enable you to form a unique relationship that will help both parties learn to make choices that will facilitate better communication. The important thing to keep in mind is that coaching is designed to help, not to hurt. By using good coaching techniques, we learn to inquire and understand others before we begin advocating or asserting our views and positions prematurely. After all, understanding each other's expectations and perceptions is the key to human compatibility, motivation, and commitment.

The Model's Design

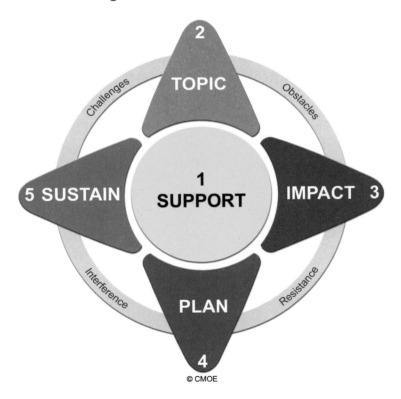

© CMOE

The visual design of the Coaching TIPS²™ Model was an intentional, creative process. The tips of the Coaching TIPS²™

Model are placed in a circular fashion to illustrate the continual, ongoing nature of the coaching process. Rarely do we accomplish all that is needed in a single discussion. Supplemental discussions and reinforcement on existing coaching topics followed by coaching on new topics will occur throughout the coach-coachee relationship. Furthermore, the series of numbered tips are not meant to imply a rigid, set order in which the tips must be covered during the dialogue. The elements are numbered to convey a general building process that offers the coach maximum flexibility and turns coaching into an art form that is unique to each coach's style, speaks to the coachee's personality, and is usable in an entirely non-sequential fashion. Any of these elements can be a starting point, depending on where two people are in their relationship or in the lifecycle of a particular topic.

For example, if there has been ongoing dialogue or a series of meetings on a given topic, the coach might start by providing some initial support and then move on to reviewing progress using Tip #4: Plan. It would be just as logical to begin with Tip #5: Sustain to engage the other person in a discussion of the outcomes and then celebrate success on the progress that has been made thus far. The coaching process has a "floating" starting point. Even though this is the case, Tip #1: Support is the core element for every coaching interaction; without it, a meaningful, collaborative coaching dialogue cannot unfold; the importance of Support cannot be overlooked and it must be present in the dialogue at some point. Similarly,

> **Expressing support should be a core element of every coaching interaction**

when coaches hit a "snag" in the conversation, they can retrace their steps to a certain point in the conversation and pinpoint the tip that may need some additional attention. This will help the coach and coachee achieve a rich dialogue.

Although using the Model sequentially is certainly not a requirement (and may not make sense in a given situation), each tip is numbered and can be used one right after the other, with the preceding tip contributing to the effectiveness of the next tip. Take, for example, the use of Tip #1: Support, and how it is used to build up to Tip #2: Topic. When beginning coaching conversations, it is highly beneficial to help coachees feel secure in the relationship and set them at ease by sharing some practical, supportive comments and helping them understand that you are opening a coaching dialogue with their best interests in mind. Ensuring that the coachee feels secure early on in the conversation is especially helpful as the coach begins to move into Tip #2: Topic, because at this point, the coachee may feel vulnerable—particularly if the conversation has lacked support up to that point.

We want to be explicitly clear that, while we have thoughtfully designed the image of the Coaching TIPS²™ Model, the Model does *not* clearly indicate the relative importance of each tip, nor does it reflect the time and effort that each tip typically requires as the conversation progresses. For example, Tip #5: Sustain, is a time-intensive part of the coaching process that can't be accomplished all at once. Despite this fact, this tip is the same size and shape as the other main tips in the Model. Additionally, we have found numerous communication behaviors and skills that lead to an effective coaching discussion. However, not all of these behaviors are fully captured in the Model. In some cases, the identified tips contain additional layers of meaning. For example, in Tip #2: Topic, an agenda that both parties are comfortable with is needed, yet it must also incorporate the more global vision the parties are striving to achieve. Combining these two ideas into one label or phrase does not fully convey the skills or tasks involved.

Finally, when thinking about the Model, try to envision your coaching situations as a combination lock; each tip of the Model represents a number in the combination, and each situation you encounter may require a slightly different code or combination. The solution will depend on the people involved. For each person and set of circumstances, you will have to figure out the precise pattern to unlock a win-win solution with the coachee. The combination is always changing. Listen to the signals, get to know the coachee, learn the code, relax, don't force it or push too fast, and simply trust the Model. Remember, coaching is a learnable skill, not a genetic "gift" that some people have at birth. The Coaching TIPS2™ Model is a highly effective communication framework, but it is not a magic wand. It simply may not work in some situations. The coaching process must be examined as just that—a *process*—and not as a single event. It requires significant patience; it's not a "quick fix." When you do find the right coaching combination, you can learn from the past, prepare for the future, and truly live in the present and take advantage of coaching opportunities.

So, let's get started with a quick overview that will give you a flavor of each of the tips. This orientation will provide you with a foundational understanding of the Model that will help to orient you as we dive more deeply into each element of the coaching process in subsequent chapters.

Tip #1: Support

Tip #1: Support truly is the center of the coaching process; it is the element that links the individual components of the Model together into a cohesive whole. The "Support" element of the

Coaching TIPS²™ Model is equivalent to Main Street or Center Plaza on a city map—it's the common thread that runs through-out the entire process. You can have many kinds of relationships with people, but if support doesn't reside at the core, you simply won't have a coach-ing-oriented partnership based on trust, respect, and candor, meaning that people will feel a little more anxious, defensive, and confrontational. Over and over again, our research confirms the necessity of support. In order to be suc-cessful in coaching relationships, we must have positive intentions and show through our words and actions that we are in touch with this element.

Supportive coaches are aware of the needs and emotions of others.

When you express support in a coaching dialogue, it does not mean artificially sugarcoating the topic, trying to smooth it over, or covering up key points. Jenny, a manager who we studied, expressed her initial perception of Tips#1: Support in this way: *"It feels like I am trying too hard to be nice when I'm coaching."* Being nice is fine, but the key is to be clear about the intent of the discussion and provide the coachee with genuine support, resources, and the skills to be effective. Honesty, fair-ness, and objectivity still need to be present in coaching conver-sations; just because you're acting in a supportive way doesn't mean you can afford to overlook the importance of sharing your point of view. Compassion and mutual understanding also have a place in the coaching process—as well as in all organiza-tions, businesses, schools, communities, and families. Support is much like the air around us: we don't actually see it, but we're painfully aware when it's absent.

This first tip of the Model not only encompasses what is said, but also the unspoken and finer points of meaning that are exchanged through alternative methods of communication, such as eye contact, tone of voice, seating arrangement, where the discussion takes place, etc. For example, giving another person some uninterrupted time and attention is a significant form of support, but it is often unrecognized or undervalued.

People often mistake open discussion and dialogue as license and opportunity to be abrasive or retaliate against others for something that has happened. An effective coaching conversation is quite the opposite. Clear and open communication may be interpreted by some people as aggression if you don't work ample support into the conversation. Although communication should flow freely, it's important that coaching conversations be non-adversarial and non-punitive. Coach and coachee are both in a better position when they set their egos and defense mechanisms aside prior to entering and during the coaching dialogue. You must make it clear that you mean no harm and that the topic or subject under discussion is not personal.

Coaching mistakes are bound to be made. It's easy to fumble during open and frank dialogue, but in these cases, giving a little extra support that is well timed is the best remedy. Abraham Maslow, a renowned psychologist, said it takes nine positive or supportive comments to make up for one offensive or harsh remark, even if it wasn't intended that way. Support is something that every coach can fall back on when things deteriorate.

Support is something that every coach can fall back on when things deteriorate.

However, establishing a foundation of support requires patience, and one cannot fill a support void with just one conversation or meeting.

Coaching is an opportunity to build constructive bridges with others. When coaching, be aware of the type of support others need and express it clearly. The bottom line is that the spirit of Tip #1: Support is trust, mutual respect, a sincere desire to collaborate, and willingness to listen!

Tip #2: Topic

As you progress from Tip #1: Support to Tip #2: Topic, you and the coachee will move quickly to the heart of the coaching conversation. This does not mean that you should abruptly change your approach from supportive to a more aggressive tone when you introduce the topic or agenda you want to explore. It *does* mean that you and the coachee both need to be at ease, share information, and reveal the facts, even at the risk of touching on some potentially sensitive issues. It is vital that the coach and coachee are aligned around the performance issue or development opportunity before progressing through the remaining steps of the Model. At times, when a coach defines a difficult or controversial coaching topic, it may indeed be shocking or difficult for the coachee, and feelings of disbelief and denial may even surface; this will usually come in the form of benign excuses and normal venting. This becomes a problem only if the parties feel the need to refute each other's points of view

When approaching the coaching topic, it is best to work from the general to the specific; to drive around the issue before trying to drive into it; to inquire before you advocate for a certain point of view or position.

on the topic of discussion and debate the feelings or excuses that have surfaced as a result of the initial foray into the coaching topic.

When approaching the coaching topic, it is best to work from the general to the specific; to drive *around* the issue before trying to drive *into* it; to inquire before you advocate for a certain point of view or position. If you successfully avoid instilling apprehension about the topic into the coachee and signal that you truly want to have open dialogue about the topic, you can obtain valuable information and an increased level of awareness. Not only does this add to the learning process, it leads to a more-complete understanding of the situation. There are always multiple sides to any issue, and a wise coach presents information clearly, considers data from various points of view, and keeps an open mind.

Clearly defining the topic is only part of the goal of Tip #2. The other part deals with revealing the overall need and deeper underlying principle that is driving the subject or topic and leads up to the conversation. This part of the discussion focuses on standards, protocols, and expectations that are linked to the topic or situation. Without some clarity around the fundamental needs, requirements, standards, or expectations, the other coaching steps or skills will merely be token gestures and superficial at best.

Individuals generally have good intentions, but they sometimes lack perspective. To help people move in the desired direction with their job responsibilities, they need feedback from a coach about how they can continue developing, what is working well, and where they need to change or improve. The spirit of this tip in the Model is one of discovery and learning, so it is important to make sure that you gain well-rounded perspective by asking good questions while actively and effectively listening to others. We can't be afraid to clearly define and call out the coaching topic as well as our assumptions, misperceptions, and biases when they arise. This doesn't mean that a coach must *agree* with everything the other person is saying, only that it's important to listen to what others have to say. We should then compare their data and opinions with our own and explore any gaps that exist between the two perspectives. This will help us open constructive dialogue and let an accurate picture emerge.

Tip #3: Impact

In Tip #3: Impact, a coach helps both parties consider the topic from a different perspective and hold up the torch of enlightenment. Tip #3 generates the deep inner power of coaching by raising consciousness and a felt need for change. With Tip #2: Topic, the focus is on gathering data, while the focus of Tip #3 shifts to broadening the perceptions, beliefs, and assumptions about the data gathered with Tip #2. The goal? For the coachee to form new impressions or become more open-minded about the current reality, practices, and perceptions. From our research and observations, we've concluded that most coaches are good at *explaining* the impact but need practice with facilitating awareness and realizations in others so that they can *internalize* the impact and become genuinely interested in the topic. One might consider Tip #3 to be the "right brain" of the coaching process; it attempts to creatively help others step back and visualize the potential effects of behavior, transcending time, position, and roles.

> **Tip #3 generates the deep inner power of coaching by raising consciousness and a felt need for change.**

Establishing impact is when a coachee begins to truly understand the impact of the situation, their choices, or their behaviors. It helps them to see the issue more clearly and with a broader focus. In some situations, the new perspective and insight that is gained may help others feel like they are stepping out into the bright sunlight after being in a narrow tunnel. With this broad perspective, the coachee can decide whether making a change, doing something new, or sticking with the status quo is the best approach. The constructive tension that is created with a broader view produces the internal motivation to change. While it can feel refreshing to look at the situation in a new light, it can also create some discomfort. Coachee and coach alike are jointly beginning to mentally move outside of their comfort zones. Coachees who work through the discomfort that must take place will generate new perspectives before taking any concrete actions or making decisions. Similar to our eyes adjusting to bright light after being in the dark, the coachee may need some time to truly see the impact and accept it. Rather than hoping to successfully establish impact in a single coaching discussion, remember that this may take some time.

Like all of the tips, Tip #3: Impact has two sides. Both parties must cease to see only a partial view of the current reality. Our perceptual maps and beliefs about the situation are always a bit out of focus. True development occurs when our introspection and curiosity are engaged. When people recognize and appreciate the impact of their actions or choices, their willingness to change and adapt is also likely to increase. With new and deeper insights, our past assumptions and perceptions can be reviewed. This will help us determine what we can do about them in light of what we truly want and are aiming to achieve. You can see the same phenomenon at work when you help people understand the implications of achieving something great. Helping them grasp the meaning of a big success can help them learn how to repeat the behaviors, share them with others, and sustain them over time.

Tip #4: Plan

When working through Tip #4: Plan, we believe that the coach should *initiate* or lead the discussion into creating an actionable plan for addressing the coaching topic, but ideally the coachee will *produce* a significant part of it. The goal of Tip #4: Plan is not only to seek immediate, "technical" solutions to problems or opportunities, but also to seek out long-range opportunities that will help develop the coachee's skills and confidence and enhance his or her self-esteem. This means that the coach and coachee are co-producers of the solutions and action plans that come as a result of the coaching conversation.

The coach and coachee are co-producers of the solutions and action plans that come as a result of the coaching conversation.

Keep in mind that in the nature of a true coaching dialogue, you cannot come up with a solid plan, decision, resolution, or agreement until you and the other party have successfully traversed Tip #2: Topic and Tip #3: Impact. It is important for coaches to avoid manipulating others or tricking them into thinking that the suggested plan is theirs when it isn't. Great coaches dedicate time in the discussion to jointly developing the plan and considering different ideas, solutions, and options.

Initiating a plan involves being willing to have a collaborative discussion, asking critical questions, and discovering all of the possible answers. Using guided questions, the coach can activate a dynamic brainstorming session on how to sort out the best decisions, options, and strategies for the coaching topic. As a coach, there are times when you need to be more prescriptive with the plan and other times when you will pioneer or champion some initial ideas and become a catalyst for more and better ideas for the future. The key with this tip is boundary leadership: helping coachees figure out the legitimate constraints, resources, and objectives of a plan, and then setting them out on the journey to success.

Most coaches, both experienced or less so, find Tip #4: Plan to be an intuitive stepping stone in the coaching process. It is typically the part of the coaching discussion that everyone likes the most and usually consumes the most time. However, a common mistake is for the coaching partners to develop an attractive plan of action but conclude the coaching conversation before the coachee's level of commitment to the plan has been verified. People can do amazing things; the question we must ask is *will* they? Whatever decisions, conclusions, plans, or agreements are made, there needs to be clear, articulated commitment to ensure

> **The key with this tip is boundary leadership: helping coachees figure out the legitimate constraints, resources, and objectives of a plan, and then setting them out on the journey to success.**

that the plan moves forward. Even if the coaching partners decide to consider the situation further or leave things as they are, some acknowledgment is needed. Thus, the final component (and perhaps the most important part) of Tip #4: Plan is the process of building commitment; success in this area depends largely on how well the other tips in the Model have been covered.

If the Support, Topic, Impact, and Plan have been addressed well, establishing the coachee's commitment to seeing the plan through may be as simple as asking the question. If the prior tips have been a struggle, securing a firm commitment is crucial

If the Support, Topic, Impact, and Plan have been addressed well, establishing the coachee's commitment to seeing the plan through may be as simple as asking the question. If the prior tips have been a struggle, securing a firm commitment is crucial and will take more time, patience, and skill.

and will take more time, patience, and skill. Verifying that everyone is prepared and has the conviction to make something happen begins with you: looking at your own passion for your part of the plan and what you can personally contribute, and then checking their commitment level. As a coach, when you reveal your own commitment to and enthusiasm for the plan, you increase the likelihood that the coachee will follow through on any necessary changes.

Tip #5: Sustain

Tip #5: Sustain is the final tip in the Coaching TIPS$^{2™}$ Model and the reason that the letter "S" in the TIPS$^{2™}$ acronym is squared; one "S" is for Support and the second "S" is for Sustain. The "Sustain" element of the Model represents the coach's intention to keep the coaching process going long after the initial conversation begins. Essentially, Tip #5: Sustain is the coach's follow-through and action behind commitment. The question this tip seeks to answer is, *"How can the parties keep helping, teaching, and supporting each other in order to make the plan and the relationship work?"*

At its most basic level, this tip gives the parties involved an opportunity to review and rehearse the steps in the action plan that will be taken immediately. From a broader perspective, this becomes the ongoing opportunity to reinforce a healthy relationship. As you bring the coaching conversation to a close, the parties need to agree to a specific time and place for the next discussion in order to celebrate and review the progress, changes, and improvements that are needed. Celebration and positive recognition is the key to this tip: the parties need to recognize and celebrate the first steps toward progress. Some people have shared with us that they believe this tip is the *beginning* of coaching, rather than its end.

The question this tip seeks to answer is, "How can the parties keep helping, teaching, and supporting each other in order to make the plan and the relationship work?"

Interference, Challenges, Obstacles, & Resistance

While every coaching opportunity will be different, chances are that at some point in the dialogue, the coachee will express some form of resistance, reluctance, or even anxiety. This can greatly affect the outcome of the coaching efforts and, if left unaddressed, may hinder the plan from moving forward. Whenever we are dealing with important plans, topics, and agreements, there is likely to be some hesitation and resistance to future and unknown courses of action. Excuses, resistance, and complaints can show up at the beginning, middle, or even the end of a coaching conversation. We recognize that from the coachees' perspective, acting on new initiatives can be daunting and often makes the coachee feel like he or she is taking a leap into the unknown. It's the responsibility of the coach to confront these challenges when they arise to help free the coachee from their paralyzing grip. Addressing Interference, Challenges, Obstacles, & Resistance takes courage, as it requires the coach to point out "the elephant in the room." This also requires understanding and flexibility. Challenges and obstacles often force us to rethink the nature of the plan and collaborate on something that is workable for all parties involved. The presence of resistance likely means that an important underlying issue needs to be addressed. For example, perhaps the coachee is experiencing fear related to moving into new territory. As a coach, it is important to stay in touch with your own reservations and excuses, in addition to those of the other person—even though other people's resistance is easier to see than your own. The way we manage these is to surface or call out those reservations and direct the interference back to the plan, where we can generate preventative measures and contingencies that will help alleviate the resistance, fear, or conflict that has presented itself. We must also reassure each other through offering support, encouragement, and confidence that we can work through any obstacles we may face.

The Meaning Behind the Model

As you look over the Coaching TIPS²™ Model, you may notice that each tip is a different color. These colors weren't chosen at random. Rather, each color choice was intentional, designed to be a visual reminder of the purpose of the tip, as well as the emotions that the tip may create for both the coach and coachee. Take a minute and visualize yourself sitting outside on a park bench on a pleasantly warm day. Imagine closing your eyes, tilting your head back, and letting the sun shine down on your face. How would you describe the feelings that the sun and your environment evoke? You probably feel calm, relaxed, safe, positive, etc. Now look at the Coaching TIPS²™ Model. Notice that Tip #1: Support appears in the center of all the other tips. The Support element is circular in shape, colored a sunny yellow, and appears larger than the other elements of the Model. These design choices were all purposeful, an attempt to visually remind the coach of the feelings that you should create for the coachee when you demonstrate supportive behaviors. The message should be that of acceptance and genuine care and concern.

Tip #2: Topic moves us from the yellow warmth of Support to an intense red. The red shades of Tip #2: Topic and Tip #3: Impact are highly visible in the Model. Even though all of the triangular tips are the same size, the Model feels visually heavier on the red side because of these bold colors. It helps coaches remember to focus plenty of attention on these critical tips and have the courage needed to slow down and ensure that the coachee is clear about what the issue is and the impact it will make. During the portion of the conversation that concentrates on the red-colored tips, the discussion could heat up, which is okay as long as the topic doesn't boil over. The tension that may arise during the red-colored tips can be good, so long as the coach is willing to carefully address underlying emotions, patiently and calmly work through any resistance related to the topic, and only move forward once the coachee has shown a true understanding and acceptance of the topic.

The blue color used for Tip #4: Plan was chosen to represent blue skies and the notion of moving forward into the future with the sky as the limit. In this tip, the discussion becomes exciting and full of optimism for both the coach and coachee. Here, they consider and brainstorm the possibilities for change and how to accomplish goals.

Bright green was chosen to depict Tip #5: Sustain to indicate that the coaching discussion doesn't end at this time—in fact, this is when it begins to really grow and bear fruit and often where it becomes the most rewarding. Once coaches reach this tip, the coaching discussion gains real traction. The coachee starts to move forward with mobilizing the plan of action and continuing the change efforts. As a coach, you have the opportunity to inspire and motivate the coachee when setbacks or failures arise, the chance to work alongside the coachee and sort through difficulties along the way, and the honor of observing and sharing in the rewards of positive behavior and hard work.

The final element of the Coaching TIPS²™ Model is the pale, tan-colored ring that appears behind all of the other elements. The placement of this element of the Model's design was intentional: Interference, Challenges, Obstacles, & Resistance can occur at any point during a coaching conversation and need to be addressed as soon as they are detected. As such, the coach needs to be ever-aware and alert to the signs and signals that indicate Interference, Challenges, Obstacles, & Resistance may be looming in the background.

In our Coaching Skills Assessment, people consistently rate the question "How important is coaching to your success?" highest when compared against any other question we ask. As you get in the habit of regularly using the Coaching TIPS²™ Model, people you coach will be more responsive and accustomed to your approach to coaching. People want to be treated as a coaching partner. They believe it enhances their performance, commitment, satisfaction, and future opportunities. And yet, despite the desire people have to be coached,

People want to be treated as a coaching partner. They believe it enhances their performance, commitment, satisfaction, and future opportunities.

you may encounter some initial resistance to your coaching overtures. For example, people who have grown accustomed to a command-and-control style of leadership may be hesitant to engage in a coaching-type partnership. They may have adjusted to a relationship characterized by power and authority, becoming dependent on the leader and only marginally interested in feedback and personal growth. The coaching approach may evoke a sense of trepidation in them when it comes to decision-making, action-planning, and problem-solving. They may also erroneously perceive coaching to be a fad or an attempt at patronization when their previous experience has been primarily with more abrupt or forceful tactics. Trust the process. Over time, your coachees' resistance will gradually evaporate as they experience a practical coaching style and the genuine values that reside deep inside the Model.

A Closer Look at the Coaching TIPS²™ Formula

The next chapters in this book are dedicated to exploring each element of the Coaching TIPS²™ Model in more detail and providing specific guidance on how to coach others using this proven process. As you read, take time to reflect on and digest the various facets of the Model. Notice how the individual tips work together. Consider keeping a coaching opportunity of your own in mind as you read and try to envision how you might use each tip in your particular situation.

If you want to be the type of coach who challenges and inspires your team members, you should learn and understand the five tips; the process can be relied upon again and again. In his book *Outliers: The Story of Success*, author Malcolm Gladwell describes his 10,000-Hour Rule as a key to becoming an expert at a skill or task. Gladwell's rule is based on the research of psychologist K. Anders Ericsson. Both individuals argue that extended, deliberate, and high-concentration practice is required to achieve mastery. Coaching is no different. Like experts in other areas, you must also be committed to learning and practicing the fundamental skills that make up coaching; continued growth and development is a crucial component of effective leadership and your commitment to learning and using this coaching process successfully will repay you in spades.

CHAPTER

3

Tip #1: Support

"As the sun makes ice melt, kindness causes misunderstanding, mistrust, and hostility to evaporate."
—Albert Schweitzer

Support is the first element of the coaching process—not because this is where you must start a conversation (although it is often a good place to begin), but because the other elements will only be effective to the degree that "Support" is firmly rooted in the relationship and discussion. Support is at the heart of coaching, both literally and figuratively, and as was mentioned in the previous chapter, is purposely placed in the middle of the process due to the key role it plays in setting up and triggering a positive experience while coaching others on important and challenging topics. In a coaching conversation, Support can be woven in throughout the interaction in a variety of ways. As you continue through this chapter, you will discover that it is possible to strike a healthy balance between being a genuine, concerned, and trustworthy partner, while also efficiently meeting outcomes and accomplishing the goals that you need to achieve.

Sometimes we are asked whether Support is more important than the other tips. As far as we're concerned, this is like asking whether eyes are more important than ears, or whether the heart is more important than the brain. The elements of the Coaching TIPS²™ process are highly interconnected, mutually reinforcing, and play an important part in all types of coaching conversations. Just like a seed needs fertile soil, sunlight, water, and proper drainage to grow and develop, all the elements of the Coaching Model are needed for a coaching experience to be effective and for people to grow. Without Support and trust, relationships won't grow and develop and the coaching interactions will be pretty superficial and mechanical.

Support: A Universal Need

The essential role of the Support element is to create a positive connection between the coach and coachee and help others understand what is driving their achievements and what they mean to the organization. The coach must demonstrate a commitment to supporting the interests of the other person as well as the organization. When the goals and intentions of the person you are coaching are in alignment with the mission and goals of the organization, it is easier to convey Support. However, when mission alignment is not as strong, the coach may have to think about and search a little harder for ways to create a supportive foundation for a positive dialogue.

You may be wondering whether showing Support requires the coach to take specific actions or if it is simply the ambiance or climate around the conversation or relationship. In reality, Support is both. It requires specific communication behaviors from the coach, as well as good timing, confidentiality, optimism, and tangible resources to reinforce a plan of action and make a discussion inviting and constructive.

As simple as the concept is, thousands of observations have led us to believe that actually expressing some type of Support verbally or having a supportive mindset can be difficult for many people. This can be especially true if you are in a managerial or leadership role and required to be simultaneously focused on people and results. Nonetheless, demonstrating Support on an ongoing basis plays a big role in both a healthy relationship and a healthy organization. It sets the stage to work on big opportunities as well as tough challenges.

Demonstrating Support on an ongoing basis plays a big role in both a healthy relationship and a healthy organization.

Support occurs both verbally, through the words we choose, and physically, through body language and eye contact, attentive listening, being present, and (most importantly) genuinely caring about the person and the overall outcome for all stakeholders. Extensive research has been done on non-verbal communication. One of the best-known studies in this area was conducted by Ray Birdwhistell and presented in the book *Kinesics and Context: Essays on Body Motion Communication.* (Philadelphia: University of Pennsylvania Press, 1970). Birdwhistell states that "words carry no more than 30–35% of a conversation or interaction, which leaves us with a non-verbal communication percentage of 65–70%...and that the non-verbal part mainly works supplemental to the words, enforcing the spoken message." What this means is that non-verbal cues and nuances are ever-present in a spoken message and are an important consideration when expressing Support to the people you are coaching.

People may be more willing to do what is expected if they can sense the fundamental trust and confidence their leader has in them. When a coach seems abrupt, adversarial, insensitive, uninterested, impatient, or uncaring, the person being coached will be less likely to respond in a genuine and sincere way. Most people have experienced negative environments at work where they felt uncomfortable expressing their opinions, disclosing development needs or problems, or taking a risk and experimenting with some new skills or behaviors. The purpose of the Support element of the Model is to create the conditions where people feel comfortable with the idea of receiving and giving feedback and having an open, transparent dialogue. People in the organization basically need to understand three things:

1. When they are "on track" and why
2. When they are off track and out of sync with the strategy of the organization
3. What they can work on now to continue being on track in the future

Psychologists Marcial Losada and Barbara Fredrickson report that in a widespread study of large organizations, individuals who experience a 3:1 ratio of positive-to-negative behaviors in business meetings are more engaged and motivated in their work. That's what great coaches want from their colleagues: a desire to learn, explore, and act with renewed passion.

When discussing the role of Support in coaching, a manager we worked with said, *"I don't need support because I get love at home. If members of my team need support, they should get it at home, too. The only place they will find compassion around here is in the dictionary."* That is a pretty cynical perspective, and whether this individual cares to admit it or not, virtually everyone needs and wants Support and wants to be validated and appreciated, particularly by a leader. Unfortunately, many people in organizations of all types are uncomfortable because they feel Support is incidental and doesn't add value, or even that it is too "touchy-feely." Never once, in all the companies we have worked with, has someone said, *"I don't like working for my leader because she gives me way too much reinforcement, makes me feel valued and appreciated, and is overly concerned about my needs."* Instead, what we typically hear are complaints about leaders who are insensitive, negative, overly controlling, and focused solely on business results. The gains that can come from Support far outweigh the risks of "going a little over- board" or being too generous with it. Your team members and colleagues deserve as much, and a vast majority of the time, they will appreciate your genuine intentions.

Support for Individuals

The key to providing genuine Support is to do what works for you and the person you are coaching. Take the time to pay attention and ask the people around you whether they feel trusted and valued; ask them if they have opportunities to talk and learn when things are going well and when a change is required. Get to know the people you lead and dis- cover the best way to demonstrate that you are sincere about open di- alogue, candor, trust, and fairness.

Astute coaches should have the presence of mind to know what type of Support and how much needs to be infused into each situation.

In some cases, people you coach may not appear to readily acknowledge or value the Support you give them. Remember that each person you encounter will have different Support needs, preferences, and styles. Astute coaches should have the presence of mind to know what type of Support and how much needs to be infused into each situation. They will give Support some thought before a coaching conversation and focus enough energy during the conversation to ensure that the other person senses a safety net when important or delicate topics are brought up.

Keep in mind that the way Support is shown and shared should be tailored and focused on what the other person needs rather than what the coach needs or might find personally appealing. Depending on the personality, temperament, and cultural orientation of a given individual and based on the situation, a coach needs to be flexible and prepared to be more or less supportive. That's part of the challenge of coaching: diagnosing the situation and tailoring your message even when it might feel peripheral or unnecessary to you. Making adjustments in the way you provide Support will ensure that your associates get the most out of the unique learning moments you'll have with each of them.

As you coach others, you may discover that some people seem to need endless support, and one coach acting alone cannot possibly be expected to provide all the support that this type of person requires. If people depend exclusively on only one or two people for Support, the people providing it can soon become fatigued. One of the most helpful ways to assist and enrich the experiences of your colleagues is to encourage them to develop a "culture of support" where there are multiple sources of support from mentors and coworkers in many parts of the organization.

Support is especially important in the coaching process when your team members are being stretched beyond their comfort zones by heavy work demands, exciting challenges or difficult problems, changes occurring in the organization, or painful mistakes. This is when Support is needed the most and because of the chaos, turmoil, and preoccupation with big challenges, the coach may overlook the need. Support enables members of the organization to experiment with new behaviors and take smart risks without fear of punishment or trouble. It ensures an environment of constructive accountability that allows people to learn, grow, and solve problems. Support gives members of the organization the reassurance that they have a partner who will be there to offer advice and assistance and act as a source of encouragement when adversity or challenges arise. It also provides inspiration and insights when facing setbacks as well as celebrates, leverages, and reinforces both large and small accomplishments along the way.

Being Directive and Supportive

The key to good partnerships and good interactions is *balance*. Support must be balanced with candor and transparency about opportunities for learning, growth, and improvement. An imbalance in favor of Support can be pretty harmless, but the absence of Support can cause others to feel undervalued, unappreciated, and ultimately disengaged. The art of being both straight-forward and supportive is a skill that is not widely practiced because on the surface, they may seem to be polar opposites. We, however, see many exemplary coaches who are able to find the balance nicely. These coaches are clear and direct—as well as being supportive and showing concern for others. In a coaching dialogue, leaders know when to inject more

Support into the conversation and when the situation requires firmness and clarity. If you focus too hard or too soon on a difficult or sensitive coaching topic, fear or defensiveness can occur, causing constructive openness to disappear. The coachee may sense rejection or criticism if the coach is overly directive. Balancing Support and consideration with candor and openness requires a bit of judgment. Otherwise, Support can be mistaken for indecisiveness, lack of resolve, or avoidance of tough issues by the coach. This is not an either/or proposition. With a bit of emotional self-management, you can and should make specific points, articulate clear expectations, share feedback openly and honestly, and be equally precise and clear about aspects of the other person's performance results, methods, or behaviors.

Your intentions and the manner in which you communicate your message determine the interaction's ultimate meaning. Are your intentions to help or hurt; to be inclusive or exclusive; to explore or dismiss; to learn more about the situation or to control the discussion? By being direct, you are implying, "This is the best way to make our conversation productive." If this is in fact your intention, calmly convey that message to the other person up front. When you communicate directly about problematic issues, do you do it in a way that maintains the other person's dignity and worth? When you do have to take a stronger position, when you have to say "no" to a request or make a required change in a plan of action, you should explain why; provide some insight into your logic and reasoning. You can explain that you are not trying to make this a personal attack, rather your position is based on your assessment of the situation and overall requirements and needs—nothing more and nothing less. Either ignoring the necessity of Support or being downright non-supportive will fuel the doubts and concerns of the other person. They will tend to pull back, contribute less and learn less, or debate with you and resist adopting a solution.

When you feel the need to be direct and assertive when broaching a difficult coaching topic, be clear and leave no doubt about the Support as well. Don't make Support an afterthought; speak your mind directly and let the other party know, in no uncertain terms, what you appreciate in him or her and what is working, as well as what needs to be changed. When this supportive foundation is well-established, the discussion of core, difficult, or sensitive issues will surely be more productive. In fact, once your partner knows that you mean no harm and that you are actually in favor of working through the situation together, he or she is more likely to follow your lead, guidance, or counsel. When you support *people* and confront *issues*, you will be amazed

> When you support people and confront issues, you will be amazed at how readily people open up and let go of the hesitation or fear they may have been harboring. This approach pays big dividends in the long term not only for you, but for the whole organization.

at how readily people open up and let go of the hesitation or fear they may have been harboring. This approach pays big dividends in the long term not only for you, but for the whole organization.

The Fundamental Behaviors, Skills, and Values of Support

Let's explore some ways you might enhance your skills and abilities when expressing Support to ensure they line up with your core values and beliefs. Remember, the goal of Support is simple: establish a positive connection. You can't demonstrate

Support by sitting around and thinking about it; as a coach, you must actually "walk the talk." There are many practical ways that you can go about creating Support in your relationships and during conversations with others. Support involves a whole range of critical behaviors, skills, and values, many of which are described below.

Acknowledgement

Your colleagues may work with you because they choose to, but perhaps they were assigned to your team. In either case, view them as your partners. When you are around members of your team and others you rely on, look for and acknowledge their successes and positive intentions. Find the opportunity to talk to people casually. When you seek them out, they will more openly share with you the things they are doing to contribute to the team as well as the challenges or difficulties they are encountering. When you build an alliance, they are more likely to explain the obstacles and problems hampering their efforts. Be prepared because you may also hear some complaints and excuses as they explain their situation. However, the majority of the time, you will be able to find something positive to build on in what they tell you about their work experiences and discover their intentions and thought process. Coach yourself to keep an open mind and maintain your belief in their fundamental value as their story unfolds. As you form partnerships with those you coach by acknowledging them as people, some Support will already have been established prior to having a needed coaching discussion.

Humility

During World War II, Winston Churchill awarded Sergeant James Allen Ward the Victoria Cross for climbing on the wing

of the plane of which he was the co-pilot and extinguishing an engine fire while in mid-flight. The young man was awe-struck just being in Churchill's presence and was barely able to communicate with him. Churchill said, "You must feel very humble and awkward in my presence." "Yes, sir," Ward mumbled. "Then you can imagine how humble and awkward I feel in yours," said Churchill. Great coaches don't put themselves on pedestals and focus on their self-importance, nor do they have need for controlling and dominating the coaching conversation. Instead, great coaches encourage dialogue by sharing the discussion time and allowing the coachee to contribute and give voice to opinions and ideas, and our research findings suggest that the coach should give the coachee at least 45% of the "talk time." When coachees are given less than that, they begin to notice the discrepancy. Let us explain.

What we discovered in our very first research project was that most leaders talk too much. We believe that coaches should make every effort to avoid dominating a conversation. Generally speaking, the less you can talk and the more Socratic you can be, the better off you are in terms of getting a collaborative solution that engages others. Our research suggests that whenever a coach talks more than 55% of the time, people begin to notice that the coach is dominating the conversation. When the coach talks 65% of the time, it becomes annoying and irritating. And when coaches talk 75% of the time, they begin to lose the engagement and commitment of their coachees. Unfortunately, we see many managers who talk more than 75% of the time, and this is very dangerous in terms of achieving a successful, win-win outcome. We always like to say that "less is more," but when the situation requires you to be more involved, you can usually get by as long as you don't exceed the 55% rule.

In addition to being humble and collaborative, coaches should also avoid coming across as overconfident, absolute, or overly certain about their point of view or position. When you begin to coach a new person or approach a new topic, don't make the mistake of assuming that you completely understand every aspect of the situation. When it's practical, inquire first; give the other person an opportunity to talk and share his or her side of the story, and give yourself a chance to review or consider their observations and data. After you have listened, be provisional about your perspective on the situation you want to explore. This means you express your insights or perspective like this: *"Based on the information I have so far, it sounds like…"* or, *"I have a different perspective than you. From my point of view, I believe we need a change to the original plan."* Keep an open mind and be willing to listen and learn something from the other party. Don't let your ego get wrapped in the conversation or let your competitive instincts pull you into a negative debate or argument.

Personal Accountability

When coaches are willing to accept ownership for their own limitations or oversights, it helps foster a safe environment for constructive and courageous conversations with others. Most organizational or performance problems develop because systems, processes, and practices are dysfunctional, or because external circumstances create real issues. Look objectively at the root cause and variables that blend together to create the results that people are achieving or the gaps you want to close. When you encounter a problem, don't overload your team member with all of the responsibility or blame them when things are not going as planned. When you look at all the

contributing factors, you leave the person's self-esteem intact. As a result, they will be more inclined to help search for a forward-looking solution. Look first at the conditions, process, and procedures, and then consider personal responsibility and motives. Prior to a conversation, prepare yourself for the fact that at some point, you will need to be a little vulnerable and "own up" to your contribution to the situation or issue you are trying to resolve.

Patience

In a fiercely competitive and demanding world that is filled with uncertainty and runs at breakneck speed, leaders often feel pressure to produce superior results *fast*. Unfortunately, this can lead to a serious lack of patience when coaching and developing people. However, being impatient will create defensiveness, and perhaps even complete resistance to your coaching message. Investing in some uninterrupted time to check in with others will make a significant impact on your ability to develop, motivate, and inspire others to excel and collaborate with you. It takes time to listen to others so they in turn will listen to your guidance, observations, and feedback. Way too many hard-charging leaders don't bother to create uninterrupted time for people on their team. When you create some "time out," be patient as people try to understand the situation you want to explore and view the circumstances from alternative perspectives. Consider giving the person you are coaching some time (a day or longer) to reflect on your insight and consider options, strategies, and possible changes to make going forward. Be aware of those who learn or

> "Patience, persistence, and perspiration make an unbeatable combination for success."
> —Napoleon Hill

change at a slower pace and recognize that immediate or total change isn't always possible and that follow-up discussions will likely be needed. You also need to exercise patience as people implement the plan, take action, learn, and grow. Don't get caught up in the pursuit of short-term or tactical fixes. The goals and changes that take the longest to achieve are generally worth waiting for. Lastly, be prepared for difficult and trying conditions you are bound to encounter from time to time. Being persistent in a good-natured way will keep the dialogue alive with the end goal in mind.

Transparency

There will be many times when being supportive means communicating with complete openness and candor. Transparent and candid communication is important, especially when you are dealing with big problems that may be more challenging than simply reinforcing and extending someone's achievement or success. When the intention is to support, honesty and complete openness are fundamental, fragile elements of the coaching process—though this level of candor may not always be met with open arms by others. On the other hand, misrepresenting or omitting things such as critical facts, relevant data, perceptions, or information regarding the coaching opportunity will eventually lead to mistrust. You can't expect others to be up front with you if you aren't straightforward and candid with them. Without this essential level of openness and honesty, your coaching interactions will be superficial and ineffective.

To create a relationship in which clarity and openness are present, the coach must be willing to take the first step by being clear and open in a constructive, non-threatening way.

Modeling candor will help your colleagues understand that the coaching conversation is a "safe space" and provides the perfect opportunity to be forthright and thorough as you seek accurate understanding of a problem or opportunity; pinpointing the keys to a person's success or when they are exceeding expectations also takes a certain skillset. The people you lead and influence will learn that their ideas, emotions, and insights are welcome and necessary for business success. They will quickly see that the coach is a good source of information, and that when they contribute their own insights to the coaching dialogue, intelligent decisions and cooperation will ultimately lead to greater levels of synergy and effectiveness. The key is to demonstrate the value you see in their perspective first. We like to say, "inquiry before advocacy." See what level of candor and insights they are willing to offer in the initial stages of the conversation and then dive deeper and be more direct when required. Explain to them that your openness and directness is not an attack on them; your intention is to attack the topic objectively and clearly, with no ambiguity.

Genuineness

Whether Support is something that comes easily for you or not, it ultimately has to come from the heart. You can't get away with pretending to be supportive for long. The people you work with will eventually see through your facade. Also, Support cannot be a predictable ritual or mechanical set of behaviors you follow. People around you constantly form impressions about the nature, extent, and sincerity of your Support. These impressions will influence their efforts and the degree to which they're willing to be open with you. Giving others cursory recognition or a "pat on the back" in anticipation of receiving some cooperation will result in you being labeled superficial or manipulative. Building a "bank account" or reserve of Support in any relationship requires time and consistency in the way you operate and behave around your team members. If you are authentic and set others up for success rather than failure, you will instill a lot of loyalty. Setting others up for success means you maintain an optimistic and solution-focused outlook, listen to their ideas, and help develop solutions that are tailored to the situation and their capabilities. When you are consistent and genuine, you will motivate action, achieve clarity, and build long-term relationships.

Flexibility

Flexibility is the ability to read or diagnose a situation and offer Support that reflects the other person's unique skills, character, and needs. As we touched on earlier, if you are to be genuinely supportive, you must be a good observer and have a solid understanding of other people's preferences and individual differences. You can build powerful relationships if you recognize what others want and need. For example, understanding their career and economic needs, as well as their emotional needs to belong, to be heard, to be respected, and to contribute will allow you to provide Support that is appropriate for different situations and the people involved in each one. Remember that some people respond positively to challenges, acknowledgement, responsibility, and recognition, but others are uncomfortable when given credit for accomplishments, especially in a public setting. In general, people have three types or categories of Support needs: Tangible (need for time, resources, etc.), Psychological (need to be recognized and valued), and Social (need to belong and be connected). A good

coach will understand, remember, and respect each person's individual differences and preferences in these three areas.

Respect

Showing respect does not necessarily mean that you have to agree with or approve of another person's logic, choices, or actions. You can respect others and support them without agreeing with them on every point. Being supportive goes way beyond a particular situation, event, or issue. Agreeing with another person's perspective is not always possible, but being respectful of their position is. As a coach, you must find ways to create a climate where others feel confident that they can safely share their point of view, data, or beliefs without feeling threatened. This is especially true when people have intense one-on-one interactions. They often report mutual feelings of discomfort, nervousness, and an increase in anxiety. This can often lead to situations where individuals become resistant, defensive, and argumentative. If fear is present, people tend to avoid feedback, growth opportunities, constructive criticism, and learning opportunities. They may also move into an aggressive stance, preparing to fight or defend their point of view. When coaching conversations are respectful and grounded in empathy, coaching neutralizes any negative feelings and results in productive solutions and stronger relationships.

Accessibility

The Support you give your colleagues can be embedded in your daily routines at work. Try to be accessible and visible to the people you are coaching. Encourage an "open-door" policy. Get away from your electronic devices, out of your chair, and observe firsthand what people are doing whenever you can. Find someone to share some good news with, seek out their opinion on an important topic, or recognize and reinforce an achievement. You should do this often enough that there is no question in the minds of the people in your team and organization that you have no ulterior motive (that you want something in return). Showing Support to your team members should become part of your character as a coach and leader, something that you just *do* without overthinking it. If possible, walk around and visit your team members at their workstations to show that you're interested in what's going on. If you work in a virtual space, have some real-time, voice-to-voice contact. Don't make them nervous but do ask open-ended questions and show your concern for the task at hand, as well as their needs. Review things like written communications, orientation documents, web and e-mail policies, online and physical bulletin boards, business reviews, log-book entries, and so on to see if the theme of Support comes through strongly enough. Then, encourage everyone to be willing to give and receive Support in order to build a truly productive culture at work. Be willing to offer members of your team periodic one-on-one time that is uninterrupted and free of distractions. Giving them your undivided attention and allowing them to bring opportunities to the surface will help you be more successful and communicate that you are open to coaching feedback yourself. You will be amazed at how much easier coaching becomes when you are willing to be coached as well.

Dedication

Influential coaches are those who are committed to consistently being supportive of their team members, both in their everyday interactions as well as during specific coaching conversations.

Mike is a great example of a leader who lives and breathes Support at work. Mike was a manager and part of an extensive study that our team conducted for a Fortune-100 organization. In it, we focused our observations and data collection on effective leadership activities and behaviors. We observed Mike's behavior for several days. We did not interview him, nor did we ask him to fill out a questionnaire; we simply tagged along with him as he went about his daily routines at work. We followed this same first-hand observation process with other subjects in the study and comparison groups. After three days, it was strikingly clear that Mike was one of the world-class leaders. One thing we noticed right away was how Mike naturally practiced Support as part of his routine when he came to work in the morning: rather than going directly to his office and responding to messages or holding meetings (as most of us do), he immediately went out into the work area and made positive contact with each member of the work group. Some of this was directly work-related—perhaps a follow-up discussion on a previous topic or a question about the status of a current project. Other interactions, however, were simply casual "small talk," where Mike showed his genuine interest in the personal lives of his team members. This show of Support was something that Mike "scheduled" into his routine every morning. During extra-busy periods, Mike was even willing to sacrifice a little of his own time to come in early and make contact with team members who were already at work. Most of the comparison group or average leaders immediately went to their offices and started reviewing performance indicators. The dedication to be a supportive, people-first leader seemed to be a major factor in the high-performance results of Mike's team.

Good Questions and Great Listening

When it comes to practicing Tip #1: Support during coaching conversations, a coach must learn the value of asking questions. In a two-way dialogue, asking great questions is as valuable as getting great answers. In fact, answering a question with a moment or two of silence and reflection on the part of the coachee can speak volumes. Thought-provoking questions enrich coaching conversations, promote curiosity about the topic at hand, and spark deeper exploration about the other elements of the Coaching Model. When coaches prepare some fundamental questions ahead of time, intently listen to the words, watch body language, and remain patient during the other person's quiet contemplation, the outcome of the coaching interaction will produce new insights and clarity about the situation.

As you ask non-threatening questions, listen carefully and express clear and non-punishing statements and opinions. You can gently attract the person's attention and may be able to bring emotions or potential resistance about the coaching opportunity to the surface early. The following questions work well to open a coaching conversation:

- *What would you like to cover in our discussion today?*
- *How are your assignments and responsibilities going for you?*
- *What is your goal for… "x"?*
- *What do you feel you are excelling at in this project?*
- *What is working well, and what isn't working so well?*
- *What has been your experience with… "x"?*
- *Can I share some feedback with you?*
- *Do you trust me to help you with… "x"?*
- *What have you learned from "x"?*

- *If you were to select something to work on, improve, or develop, what would that be?*

Just a word of caution: it is possible to carry your line of questioning too far before you offer your opinions and data. Too many questions can make the other person feel like he or she is being interrogated.

The counterpart to using good questions is practicing good listening techniques. This means you don't interrupt and you don't finish their thoughts. What you must do is provide an occasional summary and listen for the true meaning in their message. You check in to make sure you clearly understand what is being said and have a good sense of their emotions related to their point of view. You definitely don't want to go immediately into a "fix-it" mode and try to resolve a dilemma until you have given them the opportunity to share potential ideas, insights, or solutions.

Support in Action

Patrick — Take a Risk with Support

Some of the most-effective coaches make a greater effort to find ways to support their team members. One specific coach, Patrick, found that using "undeserved initial support" was a successful way to break through a difficult situation. One member of Patrick's team was unwilling to accept new changes in technology. Gradually, this team member's performance began to deteriorate until it was far below acceptable standards. The senior leadership team caught wind of this untenable situation and instructed Patrick to place his underperforming team member on a formal performance improvement plan. As he presented the situation, Patrick asked this team member

whether he would now be motivated to accept the new technology changes. The coachee told Patrick that he neither respected nor cared about the company's disciplinary policy. To
break through this challenging situation and get through to
this difficult coachee, Patrick decided to take a risk and see if
pure support would spark a change: He tore up the directive *in
front of his team member* and simply asked, "What *does* matter
to you, and how can I help to get us through this situation?"
The team member opened up for the first time, disclosing that
some problems at home were carrying over into the workplace.
He didn't know how to cope with the struggles he was facing
in his personal life and was too afraid to ask others for help. By
starting fresh with the team member—and basing the conversation on support—Patrick helped that employee make steady
progress. Within six months, this team member had more fully
embraced new technologies and was a strong and valued member of the group once again.

As this case study illustrates, from time to time, you may
need to ask yourself, "What have I done in this relationship to
create a bond and develop rapport between me and the other
person?" Developing a strong relationship takes more than
mundane, repetitive shows of Support. The previous case study
was chosen from hundreds of similar situations we've encoun-
tered, but it illustrates how Support takes root and sets the
stage for legitimate change. It also demonstrates the reasons
why we feel that the placement of Support at the very center of
the Coaching TIPS²™ Model is so appropriate.

Support as a Long-Term Investment

Giving Support to your coaching partners is an investment of time and energy. The coaching process can be compared to taking a vehicle in for regular maintenance. Regular maintenance costs some money and requires time and dedication. You won't typically see an immediate change in your vehicle's efficiency or fuel economy. Still, beneath the hood of the car and inside of the engine, all of the parts are functioning properly and performing at top efficiency. This gives the driver confidence that the vehicle will continue to operate for many years. Some owners commonly drive way beyond the manufacturer's recommendations for routine maintenance. These owners fail to maintain their automobiles because they are preoccupied, become complacent, or they can't see an immediate or dramatic change in performance. Similarly, when leaders neglect their team members and fail to maintain a proper kind of partnership support, the performance and efficiency of their team members suffers. If we are to follow this analogy to its natural conclusion, Support is the oil that eliminates the friction in your relationships. Its value is subtle and almost imperceptible! Strong, ongoing Support gives you the leeway in situations when time is limited and you have to **Support can be both verbal and non-verbal.** be direct, bold, and assertive. If you regularly support the relationship, people will be less likely to interpret your directness as aggression, insensitivity, or rejection.

Remember, support can be both verbal and non-verbal and may not show its enduring value in a fast or obvious way. As a result, short-term thinkers may believe they can treat the Support element of the Model lightly. However, if you approach your team and the relationships you have with its members from a longer-term perspective, you will see tremendous results from being supportive and showing it with your behaviors. This will help you build a team of players who are engaged, empowered, and willing to try out new ideas and add value to the business.

CHAPTER
4

Tip #2: Topic

"Failure is the simple opportunity to begin again more intelligently."

—Henry Ford

The "Topic" in a coaching discussion is what defines the agenda or focal point of the conversation. Simply put, it is what you want to talk about with the person you are coaching, which makes this tip absolutely essential to a productive coaching conversation. Coaching topics can be introduced by the leader or, even better, brought forward proactively by a team member or person being coached who senses that there is something important to explore. Additionally, coaching topics can span a variety of areas, including difficult or problematic performance issues or specific successes or breakthroughs that need to be understood, analyzed, leveraged, and repeated. Regardless of the focus, without a clearly defined Topic, the conversation will be rather vague and the best you'll be able to do is provide some

Support and continue to build an emotional connection or relationship with the other person. This certainly isn't a negative thing, but these types of conversations will become superficial over time. On the other hand, having a meaningful Topic defines the direction for a learning conversation and really sets its tone.

Because the Topic is the ignition switch of a good coaching interaction, when done well, this tip helps the coachee be more open to hearing the information you have to share, more receptive to your feedback, and more forthcoming about critical information, feelings, perceptions and ideas. Clearly this requires an environment that is absent of fear, where people can disclose honest opinions, reveal their experience and insight, and show more interest in alternative perspectives.

Because the main goal of Topic in the Coaching TIPS²™ process is to initiate a two-way flow of communication, exchange viewpoints, learn from each other, and reconcile different perceptions, we like to say that if you miss this tip, you really miss the whole coaching opportunity—but if you can tee up the conversation and set the stage by clarifying positive intentions, you have the potential for a truly wonderful conversation. Once a coaching discussion is initiated, you start down a path that can naturally lead to better understanding. With more understanding, respect is enhanced. Healthy respect leads to greater trust, which enables people to probe differences, talk about sensitive information, and constructively challenge each other when conflicts surface. Ultimately, you are able to gain full ownership of and alignment about the Topic, which places you in a better position to formulate a solution with the person you are coaching.

The whole sequence of events that occurs when you open a coaching conversation ultimately builds your bank account of trust and support with your team members and colleagues. But it does take a little planning and patience as you begin to speak into the Topic clearly and courageously. People who are firm and resolute about their opinions, pressed for time, and feel that their **People who are firm and resolute about their opinions, pressed for time, and feel that their point of view is the only true perspective are more likely to encounter resistance and pushback from others.** point of view is the only true perspective are more likely to encounter resistance and pushback from others. Another problem with being overly direct, fast, and certain with your data or assessment when introducing a Topic is that it can create defensiveness and trigger a "fight or flight" reaction. Being too abrupt or speaking with absolute certainty can cause people to either shut down or become irritated and argumentative with you. These defensive walls may be short or high, thick or thin, but with a basic foundation of trust and mutual respect, the coach and coachee can jointly break down any walls that may exist. For example, if the coachee receives an empathetic response, they may be more likely to take a step back and discover the blind spots or holes in the way he or she has been thinking or responding. In the case of a "flight" response, people may feel hopeless and find it useless to try to add an additional point of view to the conversation if you present your assertions and conclusions too hard or too fast. When you don't practice these proven skills and behaviors, people being coached are more likely to defend their position, deflect responsibility, and shift to a more adversarial stance.

Let's be honest. Even when you work with this tip flawlessly, some people will be highly receptive to the message you have to share while others will take offense to your message or the coaching Topic. Some people may have a naturally defensive or protective personality, or perhaps their past work experiences have led them to respond this way. The only thing coaches can do is try their best to set the stage and guide the conversation along. Producing good performance is ultimately a two-way street. If you can focus on the skills and behaviors you can control, your chances of a good outcome will increase.

The Topic AND the Need

There are two major aspects to the Topic of a coaching conversation. The first is its subject matter: the issue, opportunity, concern, achievement, or observation to be explored. These noticeable events, opportunities, or incidents provide the catalyst for the coaching discussion and become a springboard for the more central, strategic, or core issues to be addressed. In addition to establishing the Topic itself, the parties in the coaching process also need to explore the relevant needs, wants, results, and outcomes associated with the Topic. This is the second major aspect of a coaching conversation. Exploring the parties' respective expectations and requirements provides the context and backdrop for the subject. It is the core needs, visions, expectations, and desired outcomes that create a more complete framework for the immediate discussion or Topic. In addition to building understanding about the coaching Topic, this tip is designed to create or refresh insights into core principles and the work that must be performed. The needs expressed by the coach and coachee should come from the heart. They are deep and meaningful, and each person must know what matters most to the other person as well as the work being performed. But keep in mind that the discussion is never only about two parties; it is also about the third party: the group, organization, or owners who have a need, a stake in the quality of work and in the productivity of the organization.

The situations that indicate a need for a coaching conversation can vary widely, but the Topic will typically fit within one of the following four categories:

Development	Reinforcement
Learning or mentoring to help a person gain new capabilities and knowledge.	Sustaining, sharing, and expanding upon strengths, successes, and achievements.
Alignment	**Improvement**
Facilitating change and building commitment to strategies, goals, processes, or major changes occurring in the organization.	Elevating performance and overcoming setbacks, shortcomings, concerns, and problems.

When you discover a subject or opportunity that merits an interaction, consider which of these four categories it fits into before you begin the conversation. Remember, while giving the Topic prior consideration is highly recommended, it's important not to approach the

As you can see, the Topic can be both specific, current, tactical, and focused on the here and now as well as broad, strategic, visionary, and focused on the future.

coaching conversation feeling overly confident about the facts or thinking you have a complete picture of the coaching opportunity. With the help of the other person, you must gain some common ground before you can be certain about your data or perspective on the situation. Fully understanding what to focus on in the coaching session only takes a little time and research. Try to visualize the coaching conversation as peeling an onion, where each layer reveals more insights and information. The presenting topic, as well as the deeper underlying factors and core, root causes are all layers of the onion.

As you define the Topic for the coachee, it is important that you focus more on the tangible, observable characteristics of the Topic and less on its subjective nature. Be cautious that you don't make the intentions, character, motives, and personality of your partner the main focus of the coaching conversation. Coaching needs to focus on things people can work on, improve, and develop. It is pretty hard to change your fundamental personality, so if you unintentionally or unknowingly attack these core features of the person, you will encounter defensiveness that will hinder the mutual understanding you are trying to achieve. If you do encounter this resistance, it may serve as a hint that you may be making the Topic too personal and focusing too intently on the fundamental nature of the person you are coaching. Keep the discussion focused on key performance indicators, not so much on finding fault. Express the point that the "causes" have multiple sources, and the system/environment is at fault more often than the individual. Coaching should be more focused on doing something new or fixing processes rather than fixing intentions, character, and motives. If these are out of alignment, coaching is not the solution; you

may not have the core building blocks needed for a partnership in the first place or the person may simply not match with the requirements of the job.

The presenting topic is the opportunity that can only be seen at the surface or beginning of the conversation. It is the most obvious example, specific event, symptom of a problem, or strength to reinforce. The secondary topic that will need to be discussed is the *pattern* you see in terms of deeper issues, underlying principles, strategies, or beliefs and assumptions. Each aspect of the Topic will be supported by examples or information to help clarify the opportunity, development need, or concern to address. Let's look at the following example to illustrate our point:

> Like any work of art, you need to look at the coaching picture from far away as well as focusing on its details in order to see the whole scene for what it is.

A young, technically trained sales representative is feeling a bit intimidated by the customer's top management team and is at risk of losing the sale by not calling on these decision-makers. The sale to a specific customer is a great Topic, but the deeper issue is the sales representative's long-term effectiveness and how this person's results year over year could be negatively affected by fear of authority. We believe it is *at least* as important to look at the long-term issues as it is to examine how to close a single, short-term sale. Having one coaching conversation may not be sufficient to explore this Topic in detail. In this case, it may take more than one coaching session and gathering some additional information for both parties to be clear about the true nature of the situation.

Moving Through the Funnel

The process to help others clearly understand the Topic and the corresponding need is something we call "moving through the funnel." This metaphor illustrates how to begin a conversation about the coaching Topic. In some coaching conversations, moving through the funnel can be very straightforward and simple while in other conversations you will need to be a bit more deliberate or gradual as you focus in on the Topic. Start simply by sharing a broader observation or point of view before you rush in and narrow down the Topic to the specific details or conclusions. In the first layer of the funnel, you are trying to avoid an unnecessary conflict with or immediate resistance from the coachee by taking a fairly neutral stance. We call it "easy in," which simply means non-threatening. The coach's role is to prime the discussion and ignite interest and motivation to engage in a discussion that will eventually lead to new learning and a plan of action.

As you broach the topic at hand, you can move into the next layer of the funnel and begin to define the coaching Topic more precisely. First, inquire about the other person's perspective to gather additional information, specifics, and details about the situation you want to explore. Initially, people may act a little cautious or "closed off" and may be hesitant to provide information that could make them feel exposed or uncomfortable. When this happens, it provides an opportunity to clarify your intent and reassurance that you are simply trying to discover more objective data so there is an accurate and shared understanding of the Topic. Make sure to exercise patience and avoid blurting out your opinion or conclusion until you have invited them into the Topic. Otherwise, it will seem like it is *your* topic and not *our* topic. We recommend working through the funnel using a more "matter-of-fact" tone. We have found that when you launch a coaching opportunity with easy questions or observation points that lead to a give and take or two-way dialogue, you can create a truly accurate picture of the situation you want to discuss. It could be as simple as saying, *"Maria, how is the new project going?"* We call this "humble inquiry."

If you feel you need to be more direct to suit the situation better or because the other person wants you to call out the Topic directly and "cut to the chase," go ahead and lay out your point of view or opinion. This is the third layer of the funnel. You could start by saying, *"Here is my point of view."* Then, describe your perspective on the situation and ask them if it seems accurate. Use your discretion when deciding whether to go straight to the Topic or to more deliberately move through the funnel by inquiring before you advocate a definitive position. This applies to all situations, including those that are going well, moving ahead of schedule,

> You need to help others gain multiple perspectives—the long and the short view—if you are to create synergy in the conversation.

or experiencing better results than expected (and your aim is to understand why and encourage the positive behaviors to be repeated).

In the fourth layer of the funnel, you want to add the coachee's insights to your ideas and test your thinking and rationale. As you move deeper into the core of the Topic, test the waters by revealing your data openly and sharing your observations candidly. Again, our advice is to be a bit provisional rather than overly certain about the nature of the situation. At this point, you probably don't have a complete picture of the facts or all the background information you need. Ask them to share their interpretation of the data coming to light. Some people are perceptive and can begin to connect the dots. If they can't see the Topic, you need to be more prepared to say it clearly, simply, and without malice. This is the final stage of the funnel.

From our research, we discovered that 80% of the time, the person you are coaching is already aware (at least to some degree) of the topic or opportunity you want to explore, but for a variety of reasons they have chosen not to open a dialogue. For example, they may not recognize it as a learning and development opportunity, they may believe they can manage it on their own, or they may see it as an insignificant or peripheral issue. If it is an achievement, perhaps they are being humble about it and don't want to draw attention to it. If it is a problem that needs to be explored, they may be hoping it will simply go away. Regardless of the situation, if you create a receptive environment for the conversation and build a solid foundation of trust, there is a good chance they can and will zero right in on the Topic.

If it is a simple Topic, or one that has surfaced before, it's okay to quickly move the conversation towards the narrow end of the funnel. However, if the coaching Topic is new or it has been a while since the Topic was last explored, or if the subject matter is complex, sensitive, or likely to spark strong emotions, prepare to proceed more slowly through a longer funnel to create shared understanding about the Topic. Remember that some people like to get to the point quickly, while others will need more time to digest and understand what you are seeing. Be flexible and use your judgment as you consider the other person's intentions, point of view, needs, and style as you discuss the Topic. Try to generate a good mix of what you both prefer in a conversation.

Please understand this next, critical point: if the person you are coaching doesn't see it, isn't aware, or is hiding a problem and won't identify it, you have to boldly bring the Topic to the surface. As a leader, you have to be willing to pinpoint the Topic you see clearly and accurately but without a lot of emotion, intensity, or inference. We often say, *"Let the words confront and the tone support."* Your tone of voice will go a long way and signal your objective to create a clear picture of the situation. Even when you are addressing big or problematic issues, it is important to be calm and non-accusatory. This will prevent forcing your partner into playing the role of the victim and overwhelming you with defensiveness and excuses. You don't want to make the people you coach feel defeated or like they are failures. When you facilitate information-sharing in a supportive way, mutual understanding will begin to develop naturally. You can't get to the heart of things if you get in your partner's face. The goal is to create understanding, not to decide who is to blame or who is right or wrong. As you begin to immerse yourself in the details of the Topic, don't forget about Tip #1: Support; try to acknowledge the positive intentions present. If you introduce the Topic without Support, you will come across as detached, hostile, and distant to your coaching partner. You can be supportive by presenting the Topic from an optimistic and curious position.

Some people see this part of coaching as the moment when you give your feedback and tell people exactly how it is. However, Tip #2 is much broader than just boldly sharing what *you* think about the situation and moving on to the next element of the Model. If you express your point of view with certainty, you are sharing the facts that only *you* see. It is only *your* interpretation of reality. Rarely does anyone have a monopoly on the truth, so you need to be cautious when presenting facts as you see them. In every situation, we will always have blind spots and things we don't see clearly as events unfold around us.

Ralph Waldo Emerson, while obviously a talented writer, was unaware of the skills he lacked in other areas of his life. When he moved to his house in Concord, Emerson fell in love with the orchard on the property. He spent his free time tending the trees, writing, and socializing in the orchard. Emerson sent some of his pears to the local cattle show for evaluation by the horticultural society. He was later pleased when the committee of the horticultural society asked to visit Emerson's orchard. Emerson welcomed them and presented his pear trees with pride. He was shocked to discover that they had not come to admire his fine specimens, as he had thought, but to test the soil to understand why he had produced such poor fruit! You see, some people will be taken completely by surprise by the Topic that you present in your coaching conversations. They may have absolutely no awareness that their skills need to be honed, their strengths expanded, their performance improved, or that they need ways to sustain a successful initiative. When this occurs, it is your responsibility to help your team members feel excited about the learning opportunities rather than surprised or discouraged by the opportunity to develop or improve. Everyone has blind spots. Sometimes they block or prevent us from clearly and realistically seeing our strengths or our ability to perform more effectively; other times, they may prevent us from seeing the need for development and the value of stretching beyond our current capacity or behavioral patterns.

When we share our observations and opinions, it is crucial to remember that the situation we are looking at is filtered data. In other words, we think we are seeing an accurate picture of

the environment when in reality, we are seeing only our version of it. Our story is the result of prior experiences, our hopes, and our interests. Our mind captures, processes, and distorts our point of view to some degree. Some people would say, *"Just tell it like it is!"* But with the coaching tips we like to say, *"Tell it like you see it, with all of its potential imperfections."* We want to emphasize the importance of using the tips to open up and expand the pool of information in an effort to seek the most complete, accurate, and full understanding of the situation possible. This occurs only when you invite the other person to contribute, add to, and create a clear picture of the situation and circumstances surrounding it, and it helps you go deeper in the funnel. Remember, you are not trying to establish *who* is right, you are trying to understand *what* is right. This gives everyone a chance to engage, comprehend, and even "vent" their frustrations if necessary as they get acquainted with new information or insights. A good coach helps blend the data from both parties and tries to make sense of the situation in a way that is accurate and respects all of the stakeholders who have an interest in the Topic. Coaches can easily go overboard and analyze the situation to death. Strive for an effective diagnosis of the situation without turning the conversation into an investigation or interrogation.

If you sense some defensiveness as you share your perception, you may be moving through the funnel too quickly. To help reduce any defensiveness you perceive, you may want to disclose your own vulnerabilities and contributions to the situation you are facing or inject some genuine Support into the dialogue. This will help others feel less vulnerable or exposed, especially when you are exploring controversial or delicate issues.

To coach most effectively, you want people to feel that they can help influence the direction and substance of the discussion, so avoid overpowering or controlling the conversation. This will demonstrate your ability to keep an open mind, consider new data, and accurately see both sides before funneling down to a conclusion. If you can be a bit provisional at the outset of the discussion or when sharing feedback, the other person will follow your lead. It might sound something like this: *"Maria, I have noticed that you have missed some important appointments with the team and it seems to cause frustration for your co-workers. Do you see it differently, or have I missed something?"* A statement like this will start you down a coaching pathway. You would approach it in the same way if you perceived that Maria hit the mark on a project. You could begin by saying, *"Maria, I have noticed that your project is really going well. Do you have a sense about the things that are working for you?"*

This tip is the "discovery" phase of the coaching process.

At the bottom of the "funnel" when you are coaching about a controversial, sensitive, or problematic topic, you might hear all kinds of explanations, rationalizations, denials, excuses, and so on. This is normal and occurs when people begin to feel a sense of discomfort or personal accountability. What you want to do is establish and assert the legitimacy or validity of the specific Topic that emerges from the bottom of the funnel. Your objective here is to create an accurate picture of the situation and establish ownership.

In some coaching discussions, defining the Topic and moving through the funnel can be straightforward, while at other times, developing an accurate picture can be a bit more challenging and time-consuming. The following areas outline some

important considerations as you navigate the Topic in your coaching discussions.

Seeking Common Ground

Stephen Covey said, *"Seek first to understand, then to be understood."* Tip #2 is not so much about agreeing on the Topic and the opportunity for learning and change as it is about gaining a shared meaning or understanding of the subject under discussion and any contributing factors, background, or other insights. When moving through the funnel and seeking common ground about the Topic, remember that it is

> **By exploring needs and wants, parties in the coaching dialogue can find common ground upon which to fuel the plan.**

critical to enter the dialogue in a neutral state of mind; place your judgments, conclusions, and opinions on hold. Coaches who do this with ease are what we call "faultless coaches," meaning they have elected to set aside their share of emotional baggage and are focused instead on understanding and learning. "Faultless coaching" puts the process, not the person, on center stage. In other words, these coaches look at the process and flow of events first and the intent and motive second. As Fisher and Ury say in their ever-popular book, *Getting to Yes,* try to define the parties' *interests* rather than concentrating on the *position,* solution, or opening argument. "Interests" is just another way of saying desires, needs, or your vision of where you want to be in the future. When you focus on intent and motive in a problematic Topic, you tend to point fingers and place blame. Focusing on interests helps to distance you and the coachee from the situation and allows you to adopt the role of a solution facilitator. It's often easier to describe the natural pattern of things in third person. In the example of a young salesperson, you might ask this question: *"If you were to describe the single most effective sales technique, what would you pick? Do you think it is possible to overuse it?"*

At the beginning of the conversation, making sure that the coachee expresses his or her position can be more important than having the coach express his or her own. Give them your full attention, listen carefully, and ask for their opinion. Not only will this help you learn about the coachee's perspective and understand where they're coming from, it will also demonstrate your Support of your coaching partner. Showing high levels of Support will help to ease the challenge of finding common ground and establishing a plan of action. Active listening and two-way exchanges facilitate the understanding and sharing of observations and perceptions. Carl Rogers, an influential psychologist, believed that the first of three conditions for change is "Accurate Empathy:" skillful, reflective listening that clarifies and amplifies the other person's own experience and meaning. The ability to describe physical events and data in a natural way will help discover new insights, lower resistance, and avoid denial or defensiveness, particularly when conversing about more difficult issues. Allowing others to share their perspective does not necessarily imply that you agree with it. At this stage of coaching, all data is admissible, even the tangential or benign excuses that are ever-present when you are discussing things that are amiss. Don't judge the information

Working at understanding their view of the situation doesn't mean that you must give in, accept the other party's position, or renounce your data, your experience, or your opinions.

you receive. Instead, listen to what is being said and examine the information from the other person's perspective. This approach won't eliminate adverse emotional reactions, but it *will* minimize them—at least to some degree.

Achieving shared understanding and generating data and information to create a clear picture of the opportunity can be difficult enough on its own. But chances are that you will work with people from various personalities, temperaments, cultures, and professional disciplines that will further add to the differences in viewpoint. For example, an engineer has a very different perspective from a mechanic; sales people see things differently than do marketers. Nonetheless, individuals in these two fields are often required to work together. Communicating and finding common ground can be especially difficult given the differences in the way people with different backgrounds think and work. Specific preferences and solutions tend to be more personal and emotional. The position is one specific endpoint, leaving no room for creative options. In these tough situations, it may be helpful and easier to try and achieve common ground by focusing on the mutual needs and overarching goals of both parties.

The Time Investment

Tip #2 usually takes a little more time in a coaching conversation when compared to the other tips in the Model. Time and skillful communication are needed to scope out the true Topic and extract valuable data to fully understand and achieve that precious common ground. Even when you suspect that the coachee is aware of the topic at hand, don't rush the conversation through the funnel in order to find a "quick fix."

The time spent on clarifying and uncovering the Topic can vary significantly. It may take one short conversation or several

Slow down the coaching process and attempt to create joint understanding of the events, patterns, emotions, and perceptions. Try to be patient and remember that the coachee may or may not already be aware of the topic you want to discuss.

long ones. The most common reason why this tip can take more time is because of the complexity and the confusion or frustration that can arise as parties attempt to obtain clarity about the coaching opportunity. Sometimes this is a result of one or both members of the coaching relationship needing to control the conversation or having a personal agenda for the dialogue. Too often, patience and details are sacrificed in the rush to achieve closure about the situation. Without question, perceptions will differ. In most situations, we act on the basis of imperfect knowledge. Both the coach and coachee are likely to be partly "right" and partly "wrong" in terms of what they "know" and the information they have. Allow enough time for the Topic and needs to be heard and discussed respectfully in order to prevent premature conclusions, confusion, or frustration. This involves a lot of open and transparent communication and discussion about data, observations, and perceptions. Both parties in the coaching process need the time and attention of the other person in order to express what they need to happen as an outcome of the coaching. Ideally, a coach should spend some time on fact-finding prior to the conversation and have some observations and data to share whenever possible. However, it is completely acceptable if you come to a joint conclusion that more time needs to be spent on gathering information before you move on to the next step of the Model and creating a plan of action.

The Chase Instinct

If Tip #2 is practiced in a collaborative fashion, people will view you as an authentic partner and ally instead of a controlling or manipulative adversary. As a result, they may also be willing to let you guide the learning process. You will find that they are more likely to share inside information with you that you might otherwise miss if you apply too much pressure, move too fast, or are too critical in this data-gathering phase. From our observations of coaches, we've discovered that the coach can unintentionally aggravate their partners by doing these things. A friend of ours working in the ranching business says, *"Don't flog a willing horse."* The principle applies here as well: don't spur or prod someone who is already willing or committed to change. Coaching is the process that enables the other party to open up, brainstorm, and talk freely and directly. If you push too hard, too soon, and focus too intently on the "problem" when initially broaching the Topic, you will chase the other party away. We call this phenomenon the "chase instinct." A coach who gives in to the chase instinct tries to address and resolve obstacles, overcome resistance to change, and refute all excuses. Such coaches are impatient and don't allow the discussion to evolve naturally. The chase instinct can also be a problem if ideas are pushed too hard and too fast when outlining a plan during Tip #4. Over the years, it has been eye-opening for us to see how quickly coaches move to a win-lose mindset. This often happens when information is limited or one-sided. We can even unknowingly mount an attack—and then wonder why our partners are defensive. Sometimes the barriers or resistance will gradually dissolve if a coach simply listens and moves through the Model in a steady and patient way.

Coaching on the "Here and Now" Opportunities

Coaching conversations are meant to explore what is happening now as well as what you want to happen in the future.

Unfortunately, once a coachee raises defensive walls, it can take considerable effort and time before you can break down those walls and they trust you enough to let you in.

Defining the Topic works exceedingly well when the discussion is focused on current topics or the here and now rather than the past. Coaching and learning opportunities have a very short shelf life. When you wait too long before you surface the Topic, it can feel like ancient history to the other person. This can cause resentment or lead the coachee to believe you are the problem. Focusing on past issues or even positive things to leverage and learn from can deal a fatal blow to your coaching effort and plans to help people grow, develop, and contribute more to the organization. Be willing to use the coaching process to fully discuss emerging needs and opportunities. Look at these as positive change opportunities. If you tend to only coach when critical incidences arise (a reactive approach), you may be missing the point.

There are many kinds of situations that are appropriate for coaching, but not every situation will merit a coaching approach. For example, regular performance reviews provide an opportunity to look at a broad span of time; in contrast, most coaching discussions are focused on current situations and the near future. Performance reviews are often less successful than they could be when coaching conversations are few and far between. It is difficult, if not impossible, to coach people on unresolved topics from the past. As a coach, make every effort to

provide relevant and timely coaching rather than storing it up. Doing so will give the person you are coaching the opportunity to learn and grow on a continuous basis and will make performance reviews more productive.

Limit Your Coaching Topics

Strictly limiting the number of topics to be explored during your coaching conversations is essential. It is best to limit each discussion to one or two topics *at most*. The reason being, when you fully explore a Topic and work through the other elements of the TIPS²™ Model, you want people to stay focused and not try to fix or explore everything at once. When you put too many topics on the table for discussion, it can create a lot of complexity and people may be confused about which solutions or actions to pursue. We know how tempting it can be once you start an interaction to lump multiple topics together. However, we strongly encourage you to approach opportunities one at a time and move the coaching process along as far as you can on each one before moving on to the next. As one of our clients so aptly stated, *"We are not trying to solve world hunger in one conversation."*

If multiple topics emerge, schedule another coaching discussion for as much time as necessary, as soon as necessary. You want to give all coaching topics full and fair attention, so make sure the other person knows that you are willing to do so.

Sharing Your Interpretations

If possible, linking the Topic and needs with the expectations and goals of your team and organization—in addition to the coachee's individual goals—can be extremely valuable. By outlining the vision for the entire group, you can better clarify your coaching partner's role in realizing that vision. Ask them to describe both the highlights and the challenges that exist, the "pluses" as well as the "minuses." One of our clients said, *"I am not good at fairy tales, so just give me the ending."* This degree of brusqueness is likely to shut down any openness that existed previously. Allow expectations, along with the requirements and standards that are independent of your individual wishes and personal interests, to carry a heavy load. By doing this, you don't necessarily have to impose your will on another person; let the expectations impose a will of their own. After the other person reacts and discloses his or her views, offer yours. Use descriptive language, and "own" your personal views. Taking responsibility for your position and interpretation of the situation helps reinforce constructive openness. Constructive openness is simply a level of candor and transparency that is never overly personal, not threatening in any way, and very positive in its intent. Here are five examples of how to share your interpretation and achieve constructive openness in a coaching discussion:

1. *"I think the way you shared your report with the customer was clear and concise. Did you notice their positive reaction? Do you recall how you did it, and if so, could you share your method with the other team members?"*

2. *"Perhaps it is just me, but I often have the feeling that our suppliers are unclear about the details that appear on the work orders. I know that at times, I personally become confused when I read them."*

3. *"I have been wondering if the way we currently process the re-work items will fit the company's need to keep pace with the competition."*

4. *"I am trying to envision how the customer will see these new changes given the limited information they have been given."*

5. *"What kind of numbers would you like to see for our department in the next four months? Will reaching those numbers require us to make changes? If so, what might those changes be?"*

If you can create a vivid picture of the situation in the other person's mind, it will often help to solidify what you have been thinking about. It is unfortunate that some people view being honest and open as an excuse to be blunt, hurtful, or cross. For example, this message would most likely be interpreted as a personal attack: *"Why didn't you get that paperwork completed?"* Instead, you could engage them in the conversation and depersonalize the questions by saying, *"What are some of your experiences using the project-planning template? How is the new system working for you? How comfortable are you with completing the form at this point? What role do you think it plays?"* By using this approach, you are building a platform from which you can stage deeper, non-threatening inquiries. The following example painfully illustrates this point: A participant in one of our coaching workshops said to their coachee, *"Don't confuse me with the facts. I already have an opinion."* This attitude simply isn't very effective and won't help you reach your coaching goals. In contrast, your coachee will be more likely to share the precious knowledge and information he or she has when you are patient and show a genuine interest in them than if you try to "win" the conversation or speak with too much certainty or authority. When you start from a natural and neutral perspective, you demonstrate to your partner that you haven't yet taken a final position or reached a premature conclusion on the issue. This approach will allow your partner to be more open and creative, and to feel more ownership and empowerment in relation to the issue or the plan.

Supporting the Topic

Keep in mind that each tip in the diagram touches the center of the Model. This symbolizes the point that Support plays a role in each element, including the Topic. Every step or tip presents an opportunity to bring Support to the surface as you take care of the core business in each coaching tip. Use words and body language that give your coaching partner your full attention. When you give people your undivided attention, you send a powerful supportive message to others.

As you dig into the Topic, look for positive intentions and give people credit. Too many managers judge themselves by their own good intentions and others by their actions. You will add to your bank account of Support if you acknowledge positive intentions even if behaviors come up a little short of the mark. As simple as it sounds, you can enhance the level of Support if you simply balance the talking time. If you can give the other person about 45% of the time, they will feel engaged—but when you take over 55% of the time, instead of a coaching or learning conversation, it begins to feel like a lecture. When you talk too much and listen too little, you appear to only be interested in your personal agenda and your need to dominate or control the conversation.

We should caution you that this tip has the potential to cause emotional responses and frustration. The Topic may be an opportunity that can cause good things to happen for the partnership (a "lever" point), or it may be a potential concern that needs to be explored immediately. Your role, however, is not

to be a controller, expert, or sole authority in the partnership. Coaches must facilitate disclosure and constructive openness. Good information will surface if you are patient, consistent, and supportive. If you are coaching on a difficult Topic, look for the opportunity that accompanies every problem. Seek out the lessons and insights that can be gained and applied in terms of future expectations, needs, and direction. You will gain an entirely different spin on coaching as you explore the agenda from the perspective of the glass being "half full" rather than "half empty." Pursuing this approach is more gratifying and will result in a lot less defensiveness from the coachee.

In Summary

Tip #2: Topic is a crucial aspect of coaching others effectively. You can move on to the next phase of the coaching process when both parties feel that the following questions have been answered:

1. *Do we both clearly see the opportunity, strength to leverage, or problem to resolve?*
2. *Do we both understand the goals, requirements, expectations, or needs associated with the topic of our conversation?*

Once the Topic is out in the open and in clear view, be prepared to move to the next tip. When faced with a problematic situation, don't rehash it or get distracted by excuses and explanations. All you need to do is clarify that the opportunity for learning, change, or improvement is real. And if you have a desirable or enviable situation, you need to move on to a conversation about sustaining it or helping others adopt it. Each person's individual needs and motives portray what they truly value and what they are trying to accomplish. If you ask the right questions and listen carefully to the answers you receive, you can learn a lot about your partners' intentions, motives, and needs, as well as how you can utilize those inner desires to achieve success. If both parties understand that there are gaps (or blind spots) between expectations, goals, and current performance, the chance is good that you will achieve mutual alignment and build creative synergy as you work through the other tips of the Model.

Sometimes we can't fully understand our limitations or development opportunities, or even how to leverage our strengths, without the help of a coach. By having an effective coaching conversation, those needs can be explored in a safe environment. In the end, Tip #2 is all about using open dialogue to discover the truth together. It is not about being brutally frank or confrontational—it's about constructive and sincere honesty. Truth is in the eye of the beholder, and gently, supportively, and caringly revealing opportunities for learning, development, and improvement will provide the best chance of the coachee understanding the insights you have to share and the realities you need to explore.

CHAPTER

5

Tip #3: Impact

"Discontent is the first step in the progress of a man."
—Oscar Wilde

Tip #3 from the Coaching TIPS²™ Model captures the spirit of exploration and insight; this is where discovery and constructive tension come together and form a springboard for greater understanding and motivation. If you recall from the previous chapter, the Topic of the coaching conversation can be thought of as the "What?" part of the coaching and exploratory process. Once the Topic or situation is defined and understood by both parties, you can begin to examine the implications and ramifications of the situation—the "So What?" aspect of the coaching process. This "So What?" or Impact part of the Model requires a mental shift because this is where greater awareness and deeper understanding occurs, yet it is one of the most overlooked or misunderstood parts of the coaching process. Another way to compare these two crucial parts of the Model is by relating Tip #2: Topic and Tip #3: Impact to a group of trees. If you become too concerned about the characteristics of the individual trees (the species, their size, and other features and details), you may lose sight of the fact that they are part of the forest. Tip #3: Impact helps people see the forest through the trees. In essence, you see the big picture and gain a broader perspective.

Tip #3 from the Coaching Model came to us by complete surprise during our first in-depth research study of highly effective coaches. This concept of establishing Impact was a clear differentiator that jumped out when we analyzed the observations and recordings of great coaches when compared with less-effective coaches. The naturally talented coaches were able to help people step back from the Topic or focal point of a coaching conversation and reflect on their results, actions, progress, goals, and intentions before rushing into creating an action plan or moving into the solution phase of coaching. The Impact great coaches establish seems to tap into the intrinsic or inner motivators that get people interested and inspired to take action as a result of the coaching discussion. While the Topic of the coaching conversation deals with understanding the situation or observable events, the Impact is more subtle and slippery: its goal is to create an emotional connection between the coachee and the Topic. This part of the coaching dialogue should kindle a lot of positive energy that enables the other party to take an interest in and think about the situation or opportunity in a completely new light. When people step back from the situation and consider the implications, benefits, or costs associated with the current situation, they see things differently and it sparks a desire, or even some tension and dissonance, to resolve or address the issue, regardless of whether it is a growth and development opportunity or a performance-improvement need.

There is a common tendency for people to get wrapped up in their normal routines, working hard and fast. This situation can create some natural "blind spots," things that people don't see, don't consider, overlook, or have forgotten. With Impact, the coach tries to create the conditions where the coachee can think about the situation in a new way, raise their self-awareness, and ignite a call to action. This eye-opening awareness allows the other party to see the opportunity or feel the gap between their intentions and goals and the actual results being produced. The ultimate goal is to help others internalize the need to act. This could include a need for improvement or change when faced with a challenge or a way to replicate, sustain, and expand what is already working well. The ability to see a situation more broadly and have greater awareness is a common trait held by many high-performing athletes, business people, and professionals. They have a gift for seeing the whole field. Likewise, coaches help colleagues or team members see more of the field so they can make better decisions and take the appropriate actions that will enhance or sustain performance and make a positive difference.

Once people shake up their mindset and become open to new perspectives and insights, coaches are better able to help them unleash the motivation needed to form new beliefs and experiment with new approaches. The coach's role is to facilitate that mental shift so that each person can view the situation from outside their original perspective and experience the Topic from a fresh point of view. This part of the coaching conversation should involve open dialogue and the sharing of each other's past and new perspectives. It takes courage to be willing to reexamine one's existing beliefs or methods of operation and look at multiple sides of a situation. Keep in mind, as the coachee adjusts to clearer vision, emotions that they may have previously covered up (either purposely or not) could begin to surface. They may want to defend their beliefs, perspective, and current way of operating. In order to enable discovery without creating animosity or resistance, we recommend that coaches take a cautious and slow approach at this point in the conversation. This will ensure that the coachee doesn't become paralyzed or stunned by the new perspective they may gain. Reactions to the Impact could range from excitement and wonder to denial, anger, guilt, or sorrow about leaving old beliefs and assumptions behind.

To help further illustrate this component of the coaching process, think of establishing the Impact as putting on a pair of new reading glasses. When you put them on, you suddenly see things more clearly. When you successfully establish the Impact, others will experience a similar moment of clarity: we like to call it the "Ah-ha!" moment. The benefit of these inner stirrings is that they create a heightened sense of urgency and interest in the opportunity for improvement or opportunity to sustain and build on the things that are working. This sparks the creativity necessary to either discover a new way forward or validate the current, successful path.

With a positive coaching interaction, understanding the Impact will provide the coachee with "front-end" motivation to move to the next step of the coaching process and engage in new and creative strategies for change. The key is to increase the coachee's level of interest in the opportunity or problem before you begin to collaboratively produce an action plan.

If you are helping someone make an important course correction and they perceive tension or incongruity in the current situation, they may need to understand how their actions and choices are impacting others or results before you move the conversation to the plan of action. The fresh appreciation, sensitivity, or realization that develops through this step helps you jumpstart new patterns of thinking and acting. Some people refer to this phenomenon as the "learning moment."

While Impact can do a lot to create common ground and generate alignment around the Topic, most coaches overlook, avoid, or neglect this step. Often, coaches feel like more than enough time has been spent clarifying the Topic and they feel compelled to or inadvertently skip the Impact step of the process and try to quickly move into action. For many reasons, people who receive coaching want to continue what they are doing and resist adopting new points of view. This is often referred to as a person's comfort zone. Sometimes it is simply ego that closes off the learning process and desire to change. Whatever the reason, it is critical that you don't rush past this tip. Don't assume that the Impact point has been made and understood just because the Topic has been clearly articulated. Sometimes coaches hope for spontaneous awareness or a miraculous awakening. In actuality, establishing Impact requires a little time because an important mental process unfolds between the time that the Topic is introduced and when the planning process begins. As both parties move outside of their previous mental models and examine the situation from a new and fresh perspective, their viewpoints will begin to converge. This results from both parties gaining a fuller, more accurate understanding of the differences between the current situation and what needs to happen in the future. It is a crucial part of the coaching conversation. In our Coaching TIPS²™ Model, we chose the color red for this tip intentionally. This color choice is meant to serve as a reminder to stop the coaching conversation for a moment and allow the Impact to sink in.

Helping others examine the situation more closely will allow the facts, realities, and truth to surface.

With Impact, patience becomes the first order of business. Slow down as you create some mental space for your partner to absorb the new insights and digest the meaning you are creating. This can be the start of a compelling, emotional, and transformational change in the way the coachee thinks. Remember, as you and the coachee begin to examine issues from a new perspective, you will generate a positive form of tension ("constructive tension") that calls for resolution. The hope is that a closer examination of the situation will allow more of the facts, realities, and the truth to surface.

As we mentioned before, many coaches shy away from opportunities to establish Impact because finding the right way (or a creative way) to go about it can be challenging and the transparency it creates can be a bit uncomfortable; Impact helps people fully understand the real implications of the situation and their actions. We recognize that it isn't easy to "hold up the mirror" and help others get an honest glimpse of the situation, the path they are on, and the possibility of changing the course. Few things in life can be seen with clarity when they are viewed only by one person from one perspective. The power of

coaching lies in the fact that two or more people work together to validate the facts and see the whole picture.

Landing the Impact

Getting the Impact to stick the first time around is a real boon to your coaching efforts. Experienced coaches have learned how to "land" the Impact, just like an expert fisherman would "land" a trophy-winning fish. The challenge is that, like fish, when people feel the Impact (the hook), they may resist and try to slip away. Sometimes it's easy for others to see the Impact; other times, helping people to see the Impact may feel nearly impossible. Don't expect to be appreciated for your efforts, especially not right away. It is fairly normal for people to feel uncomfortable when they see the full Impact of the situation, their choices, or their actions. Some people may even find it agonizing to deepen their awareness. We've all heard the phrase "no pain, no gain." In business coaching, we might say "no pain, no learning or change." The discomfort that comes from understanding the Impact must be stronger than the forces supporting the coachee's current choices and behaviors. Some people may need to hit bottom before they experience their "Ah-ha!" moment. While landing the Impact softly will work for some, it simply won't do it for other people. In fact, it may actually become necessary to make establishing the Impact the goal of your entire first coaching conversation, with follow-up discussion(s) needed to tackle the other tips.

Good timing, creativity, and knowing when to make your point is vital to successful learning and discovery. And please remember that the purpose of establishing Impact is *not* to "break" someone! Coaching should give the other person new

measures of effectiveness and additional insight, hope, and drive
regarding a situation, problem, or opportunity. It should be an
early-warning system that lets the coachee know a learning opportunity exists. But you can't stop there. As a coach, you can't
ever assume that people will eventually get it on their own. Try
to assess how big the Impact deficit you might be dealing with
actually is. This could be a blind spot that's big and persistent,
or you might discover that it is small and easy to address. The
key is to achieve balance. You don't need to overdo this part of
the conversation. Instead, ignite the motivation that will lead
to some change, learning, and even excitement.

Traction and Inertia

People sometimes look at a coaching Topic as if it were an
ice cube: set and rigid. To change the shape of an ice cube, it
must be melted gradually, which will make it more malleable.
As a liquid, the material can be reshaped into a form that is
more usable. The transition a coachee makes from the original
set state to the more flexible (and thus, more moldable) state is
achieved by establishing the Impact.

An Explosion of Energy

Establishing Impact in a genuine way is a truly exciting process. As the Impact lightbulbs flicker on, both opportunities
and challenges begin to come into greater focus and a whole
new world opens up within the mind of the coachee. You can
see the burst of energy within the coachee when it happens.
Despite this, we don't want to make establishing Impact sound
like an event. Impact is rarely "once and done," and it is never
completely finished. Rather, it is more of a continual process
or an ongoing journey of discovery. A coach can quickly bring

the Impact into focus, but it is easy for the Impact to dissipate and dissolve over time and for the blind spots to return without continued discussion. With regular coaching, people will maintain their clarity and motivation.

A Flexible Approach

Establishing Impact is going to be different with everyone you coach, and like the Support and Topic elements of the Coaching TIPS²™ Model, you will have to adjust your approach to reach each person you coach. To effectively establish Impact with someone, it really helps to know the person's core motivations, values, and goals. For example, a coach can ask the coachee to reflect on a given situation from a customer's point of view. This approach may only make an Impact on someone if they know what the customers actually think, and if they even care about the customers to begin with! It is also dangerous to assume that the coachee's goals and values are similar to your own. If you offer sage advice or recommendations that are based on your personal values, expect to be greeted with doubt and resistance. Until you reorient the conversation to reflect what your coaching partner cares about and link the Impact to what they are trying to achieve, there will be no "felt need" to change.

Helping people see the effects of their behavior can sometimes be very simple. One of our friends shared an elegant example of how his spouse compassionately conveyed Impact: Our friend, Marcel, has a love affair with fast, imported cars. He likes to drive them, and he likes to drive them fast and push the limits of their engineering. On one occasion, Marcel was out on a short trip with his spouse and youngest daughter, who was riding in the back seat.

As soon as Marcel got behind the steering wheel, his race-car paradigm started to settle in. With his driving gloves on, Marcel started going through the gears, and once he hit the thoroughfare, his speed began to accelerate. He didn't say a word to his passengers. He was in his element and enjoying the pure exhilaration of being in control. He was having fun because, for him, driving was a sport. It was a test to see how well he could dart in and out of traffic. In his mind, he was on the Indiana Speedway.

After a few minutes, his wife had the good sense to gently put her hand on his shoulder and very quietly express the following words: *"Marcel, your daughter is watching you very carefully right now."* Marcel's daughter did not hear those whispered words. She, herself, was enjoying the thrill of the sport. Just like Marcel, her mind was caught up. She was only fourteen years old, two years away from getting her driver's license and having the opportunity to take the wheel like her father. Marcel shared with us that the words of this coach, his wife, resonated in his mind for weeks. Nothing else needed to be said. These words created the introspection and thoughts about the behaviors and attitudes that he was inadvertently passing on to someone he deeply valued. We have always been impressed with this story and how effective, short, and illustrative establishing Impact can be when it is done well.

How to Do It

What are the possible pathways to help others become more conscious about the impact of their behavior? How do you arouse the mind? How do you shift the mindset or alter the focus of a person's current thought process? Let's explore some more possible ways and creative methods that a coach might use to help shed light on the issue in a new way for the coachee.

There is certainly no single, correct answer because human beings are all unique. Different things capture their interests, raise their awareness, and move them to new thoughts, feelings, and actions. The things that make an impact on individuals (causing their minds to refocus, analyze, and reach resolution) will vary depending on the individual's style, experience, and personality. Here are ten fundamental approaches or pathways to establish Impact with the people you coach:

1. Value Analysis

Conducting a value analysis of the situation will help you know how to increase the "felt need" for change in the person you are coaching. In a sense, you are evaluating the pluses and minuses of the other person's current approach, behaviors, actions, etc. This method works quite well when both tangible and intangible benefits and losses associated with the current approach can be seen or calculated. It helps both partners to relate more closely to the issue and will bring the Impact home in a logical and rational way as you and they see what is working and what might not be working. If, after doing a value analysis on the Topic, it appears that changing the current approach is *not* appropriate, then both parties can feel confident that the right thing is being done already—a value judgment that is based on the best available data and information. However, if the other person can see, in no uncertain terms, that the current situation or their approach is resulting in unintended costs (either at an individual level or for the team), it may be easier to see the Impact and recognize that some kind of action is warranted.

2. Short Stories

There are times when sharing examples, case studies, and anecdotes can be effective—as long as they are not shared excessively, and if the sharing is done appropriately. If the coachee can experience the Topic and Impact *vicariously* through the sharing of a story or experience, the effect may be felt strongly enough for the person to make the necessary change. You can also use metaphors or analogies to make connections and increase understanding of the Topic and its Impact.

3. Tough Questions

Using legitimate and genuine questions can be an effective way of establishing the "ah-ha" moment for a coachee. If you feel questions are the right approach for creating deeper awareness and interest, ask exploratory, penetrating questions like the following:

- *What are the results you hoped for?*
- *Each of us is looking at this from our own perspectives, but what are the other viewpoints that we should consider?*
- *What do we really need to get out of this situation?*
- *In what ways are we meeting the project's original goals and expectations?*
- *How can we look at this in a different way?*
- *What are the unintended results, positive or negative, that you are getting?*
- *What would we accomplish if everyone in the organization used the same approach that you are using?*
- *How is the current approach meeting our core needs?*
- *How are you contributing to this situation (in a positive or negative way)?*
- *How fair are we being to our other stakeholders?*

4. "I" Statements

If asking questions doesn't establish the Impact you are looking for, try using some honest "I" statements to express the points you are trying to make. When you are unambiguous and assertive, it might be surprising or even shocking to the person you are coaching. Here again, you will need to be prepared to manage the pushback if people perceive your assertion to be inaccurate or unfair. When you use this approach, be declarative. For example, *"I think that the customers are disappointed with our current level of service, and they may be wondering whether we're worth their investment,"* or *"If I were working in the other department, I would probably feel uneasy about the approach you are currently using."* Allow the "I" statements to initiate further dialogue in the discussion.

5. Visualization

Some people respond to mental images and "word pictures." In the world of professional sports, games are typically recorded so coaches and their team members can watch the recordings of their performance after the fact. Because they can review the game film (repeatedly, if necessary), they are able to learn more about the style of play and the areas in which they could improve. They discover what is really working and what can be further developed. In this scenario, the Impact comes across very clearly, and escaping the truth is difficult. Just like most athletes, some people need a very vivid, game-film-like experience. Others might actually need to taste, hear, or smell the Impact in addition to seeing it in order to consider or understand the need for making the change. In this situation, rather than asking them to consider how a customer might feel, they would be better served by actually talking to or observing a truly satisfied customer and asking them why or conversely, talking to a disgruntled customer who isn't satisfied with the working relationship and asking why.

Unfortunately, some people will choose to ignore the Impact and continue doing the things they have always done. They aren't willing or able to get out of the box; their perceptions and paradigms eclipse reality. The power of this concept came through to us one night while staying at a hotel that was experiencing some problems with its fire-alarm system. For some unexplained reason, false alarms went off about every 20–30 minutes *all night long*! At first, the alarms had everyone's attention, and all of the hotel guests responded to them immediately. However, it didn't take long before we grew insensitive to the alarms and began to ignore them when they went off. In effect, we became "impact blind." Subconsciously, we developed the mindset that we would only take the alarms seriously if we had stronger signals, like smelling smoke or seeing flames. That would become our new threshold of Impact that would then lead us to take action. Somehow, it finally dawned on many hotel guests that this was a very foolish set of beliefs, and that the price of action was really less than the cost of inaction— especially if the alarm was real. So we took the precaution of evacuating each time the alarm went off, even though it was terribly inconvenient.

Sometimes the best warning systems are inaccurate, and that is the reason the coaching partnership requires both parties to jointly consider the signals and the alarms. Together you can avoid falling into "paradigm paralysis" or other forms of denial or resistance.

The principle of Impact through visualization is well illustrated in another true story from history. At 9:30 on a July

evening several years back, a disastrous explosion occurred on a petroleum platform in the North Sea off the coast of Scotland. 166 crew members and two rescuers lost their lives in the worst catastrophe in the 25-year history of the North Sea exploration. One of the 63 crew members who survived was a Superintendent on the rig whose name was Andy Mochan. From his hospital bed, he told the story of how he was awakened by the first explosion, and then heard the alarms. He ran from his quarters to the platform edge and jumped 15 stories from the platform into the water. Because of the water's temperature, he knew that he would only live 20 minutes, at most, if no one came to his rescue in time. At that point, oil had also come to the surface of the water and ignited. Yet Andy still made the choice to jump 150 feet into an ocean of burning oil and debris in the middle of the night. When he was asked why he took that potentially fatal leap, he did not hesitate in saying, "It was either jump or fry." He chose *possible* death over *certain* death. The underlying belief is that "as we think, so shall we act."

6. Role Reversal

A "role" is the position, assignment, task, or function that you fill. Naturally, many people view their role or roles quite narrowly, and within this view, they are often thinking about themselves to a far greater degree than they think about others. This is not to say that self-interest is all bad—it's just that if it's taken to an extreme, this point of view can create an inaccurate perception of reality. We all want to be successful at what we do, but if individuals focus too heavily on their immediate personal success or become overly focused on the narrow view of their role, they may unintentionally hinder their long-term success. It is not uncommon for people to be a bit short-sighted. If you can change the point of view by reversing roles or shifting the positions long enough to see the current situation as others see it, you will be a more effective coach and raise the awareness of the person you are coaching. If you aren't able to make this shift, you may be destroying the cooperation, interdependence, and synergy that makes the coaching partnership work.

While every viewpoint has both flaws and strengths, each new insight gained will enrich the dialogue and fuel the coachee's motivation to change. Try asking the coachee to conduct a role-reversal exercise with you by asking them to envision the Topic or situation from the point of view of a key stakeholder. For example, you might explore the likely impressions and reactions of a customer, another colleague, the community, or your shareholders. You could even ask the person you are coaching to mentally switch places with you and vice versa. Sometimes a role reversal is uncomfortable, and it should be—that's what makes it work! Be forewarned that the coachee may want to slip back out of the role-reversal process just as soon as it begins. This is a normal response because the constructive tension created by this exercise can be uncomfortable. Hang in there, help reset the stage, and try it again.

7. Examining the Need

Another helpful pathway to establishing Impact is through a careful examination of the desired outcome or *need*. In this context, the "need" refers to your own goals, as well as the goals of the people you are coaching. By examining the current choices, behaviors, and attitudes from the perspective of the underlying goals and values guiding them, it may be easier to see inconsistencies and lack of congruity between goals and behaviors. For many of us, our choices, behaviors, and attitudes

are blocking progress to achieving our goals and living within our stated values. Surprisingly, the path a person is traveling and the destination he or she desires to reach are often disconnected; people often find themselves "off track" despite clearly understanding where they want to go. Maslow's Hierarchy of Needs is a useful framework for thinking about the different levels and types of human needs and motivations. For example, many people find that they enjoy feeling secure and strive to achieve it, yet they still find themselves doing things that are inherently risky. If you fail to see the paradox at work in this situation, you may inadvertently battle against the people around you who help to ensure your security. The idea here is to help the other person understand or clarify the need, expectation or goal and evaluate whether the path, decisions, and/or behaviors are contributing to the fulfillment of that need or achieving the desired state. As a coach, you want your coachees to pause and ask themselves, *"Will I reach my desired state or achieve the goals or results I want if I continue to operate in this way?"*

There is an old joke about an airline captain who broadcasted this message to passengers during their flight: *"I have some good news and some bad news. The good news is that I'm happy to report that we have favorable tailwinds and we're making very good time. Now for the bad news: We're lost!"* While this sounds funny, all too often what is occurring or what we are doing doesn't really match up with where we are going or the need to be fulfilled. Coaches help people reflect on this and use it to motivate them to make a change.

> **People often find themselves "off track" despite clearly understanding where they want to go.**

8. *Time*

Productive patterns of behavior can lead to payoffs that are distant, even abstract. By the same token, *counterproductive* behaviors can also sometimes have distant implications. As such, the use of time is another interesting way to establish Impact when coaching. If you are able to guide a coachee into mentally rolling the clock forward, you may be able to help them gain new perspectives where rigid ones had existed previously. For example, you might pose hypothetical questions like the following:

- *"In what condition might we find ourselves in two, five, or ten years in the future if we continue with the status quo and don't change?"*
- *"In what condition might we find ourselves in the future if we successfully adapt to the new strategies for future business success?"*
- *"How likely is it that our business will be the same as it is today in two, five, or ten years?"*

As you coach, you will find that some people get stuck thinking and operating either in the past or in the present. Getting stuck will have adverse and far-reaching consequences for you and the people you coach. You can't fail to factor in the passage of time. Remember what Marshall Goldsmith said: *"What got you here won't get you there."* Living in the past can undermine current relationships and motivation, which limits people's ability to make positive contributions to their work and meet the needs of their stakeholders. Similarly, if you're always fantasizing about how things might be different in the future and what might take place, you're likely to miss a lot of

great opportunities in the present. Using time, you can open the other person's eyes to opportunities they might otherwise miss.

9. The Reach Factor

You can help create awareness of the impact a coachee's behavior has by helping them discover the magnitude and range of the effects their behaviors will have or is having. This includes the reach their current actions, behaviors, choices, or performance has on themselves, peers, teams, customers, and the organization. Your job is to help them evaluate whether the current approach will yield the results this broader group expects. It can be easy to forget the magnitude our individual actions and behaviors can have on other people or things. Raising a coachee's awareness about the Impact that the Topic has on others can be a productive catalyst for change. For coachees who care about these relationships, you will spark some fresh thinking.

10. Location

The final facet of Impact is *location*. While this may seem a little bit odd or unexpected, it's possible to help others visualize the Topic and its Impact by having them physically move to another vantage point. For example, you may want to ask someone to move to another location, department, or office. From this new perspective, the coachee will be able to see alternative viewpoints and may be able to interpret the situation in a new way and come to different conclusions. If you are coaching someone about a resounding success, you can encourage the coachee to help others learn and grow and share in the success. Another example of this Impact method is to arrange for some job flexibility and encourage people to rotate assignments. This will help them see the world in a new light.

Your job is to help the coachee become more enlightened. Plato once said, "the unexamined life is not worth living." He understood the true nature of Impact. The experience of seeing the situation or Topic in a new light can be moving and very powerful.

In Summary

As a coaching partner, you are responsible for uncovering as much truth and creating as much understanding as possible, even at the risk of experiencing some tension and discomfort. After all of your coaching efforts, the coachee's heightened awareness or understanding of the Impact may still kick in gradually—or it may happen immediately. More than one type of Impact pathway may be required to spark the awareness you are seeking. Sometimes planting the Impact "seeds" can feel tedious. Unfortunately, no one can control when those seeds will germinate and help the coachee gain new insights, so it's important to be patient and let things sink in.

Ultimately, Tip #3: Impact of the Coaching TIPS²™ Model is designed to do two things:

1. Enable the coaching parties to reflect on the Topic with an open and fresh mindset.
2. Arrive at a shared conclusion and felt need that something new must happen.

Serious change and growth does not occur until people engage in introspection and gain greater awareness. Once the Impact has been established, coach and coachee alike feel ownership for the situation and are ready to jointly own the responsibility for creating new ideas, carrying out a plan, or building new solutions. Only then are the coach and coachee fully prepared to cross the bridge from discussing the Topic to creating the Plan of Action.

CHAPTER

6

Tip #4: Plan

"I learned early in my career that people are more motivated and engaged when they can make their own choices and control their own fate."
—**Dr. Steven J. Stowell**

The fourth tip of the Coaching TIPS²™ Model, Plan, is all about creating solutions and taking action! All of the previous elements of the Model have been leading towards this element of the process. This is the moment when you begin to conceptualize and then solidify the Plan of action. We fondly refer to this tip as coaching's "pay dirt."

"Pay dirt" is a term that has its origins in the mining industry and refers to a high value, rich place to dig that will create value. During this phase of coaching, short and long-term strategies for addressing the coaching Topic and need

This action-oriented tip involves deciding who is going to do what, where, when, and how.

are considered. The goal is to create an agreement that will achieve real wins for each person, as well as for the organization. This tip certainly involves creating plans and bringing about change, but at this point, the coaching partners also begin to take accountability for what comes next. The mechanics of the Plan and how to divide up the work is important to be sure, but of equal importance is the sense of responsibility for the Plan and the transfer of control to the coachee. In addition to its more tangible benefits, a collaborative approach to the Plan of action also provides an opportunity to add to the bank account of Support and trust.

Learning to Let Go

This tip requires a lot of intellectual and rational thinking, but it's also important to generate passion and drive by capturing the imagination of the coaching partners during the planning phase. This creative energy will result in coaching partners having a stronger commitment and the motivation necessary to follow through on the Plan. To successfully achieve the desired goals, both rational thinking and emotional drive are needed. You and the coachee must create an effective strategy, as well as build commitment and the willingness to see it through. Communicate your readiness to play your part in the Plan through your excitement, however small or large your role may be. Just avoid creating unnecessary dependency by enabling the coachee to rely on the coach to produce the Plan.

Traditionally speaking, this step is attractive to action-oriented managers. They have a tendency to shoot right past the Impact step and begin prescribing pre-formed plans. These coaches can become overly directive. In some coaching situations, a directive approach is appropriate. But in many situations, a coach can let go of some control of what the plan is for moving forward. The good news is most managers recognize and identify with the processes of thinking about the situation proactively, brainstorming available options, eliminating those that are weak, and envisioning the steps necessary to achieve important outcomes. Some people would argue that during the planning phase of the coaching process, this type of traditional thinking is all you need to be successful. Others can see that achieving success with a plan requires intellect as well as a sense of ownership.

One of the keys to unleashing synergy in Tip #4 is to continue the coaching process by finding shared understanding about the direction and active measures required to make changes and move forward while maintaining an honest, open dialogue. Both partners should be involved in designing the solution and must therefore relax their egos and resist the need to control the Plan and be the "expert." Consider the challenge that nature presents delicate butterflies with while they are still in their cocoons: if they are assisted in their escape from the chrysalis, their wings won't be strong enough to fly. However, if they are left to struggle and push their way out on their own, their wings will gain the requisite strength and they will survive. In a similar fashion, we all need to think and be challenged; it makes us stronger and more independent. As a coach, you may feel the urge to "help" or rescue the coachee by taking on the burden of formulating a Plan. Just remember that in many situations, "helping" too much will actually be detrimental to them. Learning to let go of pre-formed solutions can be a very challenging aspect of this tip. One way to avoid this situation is to not enter into the dialogue with plans or solutions already in mind. You are more likely to run into challenges if you try to influence or coerce the other person into thinking or doing what you had in mind ahead of time. Your only real intention should be to contribute positively to the process of creating a good Plan—regardless of whose ideas go into it. Generally speaking, you should approach this tip of the Model without an agenda, except when the Plan is a mandate and non-negotiable. Safety is a good example; in these situations, required behaviors are clearly prescribed.

We realize that relinquishing some control isn't easy for those who like to be in charge or prefer vertical power relationships. Remember, whenever you direct the Plan, you inadvertently set yourself up as the expert—and potentially as a scapegoat if things don't work out well. If the Plan you formulate fails, it will be tempting for others to say, *"I tried to tell you…"* or *"I told you so."* In contrast, when your Plan is right on target, you inadvertently reinforce others' sense of dependency on you; they will learn one lesson: rely on you to provide them with the good ideas instead of coming up with them on their own. In some respects, Tip #4: Plan is where you create real value for the organization. This is where you have the opportunity to capitalize on your collective creativity and the lessons you've learned over time. If the Impact was fully established, you should see some initial signs of buy-in or enthusiasm for taking action from the other person because they recognize the need to grab ahold of the opportunity and run with it.

Remember, whenever you direct the Plan, you inadvertently set yourself up as the expert—and potentially as a scapegoat if things don't work out well.

A Continuum of Planning Styles

There is a wide range of styles or levels of flexibility that a coach can use during the planning phase of coaching; whatever the coach decides to do will depend on the situation or circumstances. These different styles and levels fall along a continuum. Various points represent different styles to adopt as you begin working on a Plan with the coachee and to know how much you can or should let go.

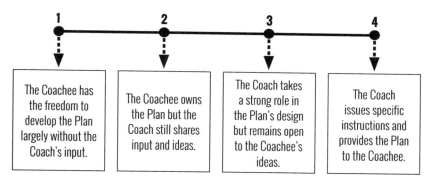

1	2	3	4
The Coachee has the freedom to develop the Plan largely without the Coach's input.	The Coachee owns the Plan but the Coach still shares input and ideas.	The Coach takes a strong role in the Plan's design but remains open to the Coachee's ideas.	The Coach issues specific instructions and provides the Plan to the Coachee.

The continuum begins at Point 1. This style choice allows the other party a great deal of freedom and discretion in developing the Plan, as well as coming up with an appropriate course of action. Selecting this style is a good choice when the coachee is competent, mature, knowledgeable, willing to learn, and/or a self-starter. These people should be empowered and encouraged to think independently and make decisions about the Plan largely independent of the coach. You might also select this style if the coachee is a subject-matter expert in the technical aspects of the Plan and you are less knowledgeable in that area. Finally, this may be a good style to use when ample time and other resources permit trying out and experimenting with novel approaches.

Point 2 on the style continuum is one of sharing your input and ideas while still helping the coachee to experience a sense of ownership over the Plan. Remember, this shouldn't be *your* Plan. It needs to be jointly developed. Even though your assistance and participation in the brainstorming and decision-making process is needed, it should be a blend of the best thinking from both parties. Walk side by side with the coachee through the decision-making process until a Plan emerges that meets the requirements of the situation. You might select this style when time and resources are available to work through a solution. This supportive style is very empowering for people and often helps coachees build confidence in their skills, abilities, and experience.

At Point 3 on the continuum, the coach takes on a strong role in designing the Plan for the coaching Topic. As a coach in this situation, you will design a fairly precise solution but will still remain open to new possibilities and ideas for improvement that may come from the coachee. When this is the appropriate style, clearly explain the Plan and guide them in understanding how to see the Plan. While doing so, encourage questions and discussion, but don't expect to make a lot of modifications to your design. If the person you are working with is struggling to see the Impact of the situation during the coaching discussion, this approach to initiating the Plan may be a good fit. Likewise, if your partner's personal needs, expectations, and intentions are out of alignment with the group, or if your partner lacks experience, then you may want to adopt this more influential style at the risk of fueling some resistance because of the direction you are infusing into the planning process.

At Point 4 on the planning-style continuum, you essentially take a directive approach. When using this style, you issue

specific instructions, provide others with the Plan you've developed, and explain what to do—with minimal discussion. This style would be most appropriate when you are in an extreme situation or during an urgent crisis, when you have no time or patience left to build the Plan collaboratively. You do run the risk of reinforcing a dependency relationship by teaching the other party to rely on you for a solution, but that may be a risk worth taking in certain situations. One warning sign that you're moving into this territory is when the coachee repeatedly asks, *"What do you want me to do?"* Sometimes this is appropriate, but more often, it allows the coachee to avoid taking real responsibility for the situation and its resolution. Point 4 on the style continuum causes your team members to become immune to thinking and learning on their own because they know the coach will save the day. Even though this approach is an option, it can be unsatisfying for most people in the long run because it reinforces a *vertical* hierarchy or power relationship. You can get by with a commanding style in some situations—as long as it doesn't become your core style and you don't use up your stockpile of Support in the process. When you are directive, others can feel devalued or marginalized.

Regardless of the planning style you use with the coachee, the outcome should be a viable and sustainable Plan that will produce positive results.

Regardless of the planning style you use with the coachee, the outcome should be a viable and sustainable Plan that will produce positive results. Generally, the more experienced, confident and committed the coachee feels, the more your style will gravitate to Points 1 and 2 on the style-choice continuum. The less experienced or more resistant the other person feels about change, the more you may need to tactfully and caringly move along the continuum towards Point 3 or even Point 4. If you choose this approach, it's because you genuinely feel it's needed and believe that the advantages of exerting more influence over the Plan offset the long-term disadvantages of causing potential resistance or defensiveness in the other person.

Evolution of a Solution

When developing a joint solution, which will likely be the most common style you use, think of Tip #4: Plan as an evolutionary process that moves from one stage to the next:

Stage 1 – start with each party's initial ideas
Stage 2 – try to facilitate new or emerging synergistic ideas
Stage 3 – consider merging the ideas
Stage 4 – settle on final ideas and active measures to take

Skilled coaches believe that when developing solutions, two heads are better than one. You will experience more success with this tip if both parties are willing to keep their minds open and explore new possibilities to augment their ideas or solutions. As a coach, your role is to be a catalyst for creativity, brainstorming, and risk-taking by encouraging the other person to start fresh, challenge conventional thinking, and stay open to new possibilities. You can do this by looking for ways to turn differences in objectives, needs, and skillsets into collaborative strategy. Focus primarily on facilitating the thought process and not advocating for your preferred solution. Ask your partner, *"What do you think we might do now?"* During the discussion, use some of the following questions to open a dialogue about new options and approaches:

- *What do we need or want to have happen?*
- *What goals, results, and objectives should we focus on?*
- *What resources do we have to work with?*
- *What constraints and requirements do we need to work within?*
- *How flexible are these constraints?*

Once you ask the prompt question, use your active-listening skills. Then you will be in a place where you can begin inventing and brainstorming on new or original options. Good judgment and balanced thinking are critical during this stage.

After this creative phase, you can begin to formulate a precise "flight plan." This is where you get very specific and work out the details. Some coaches call it the SMART Plan: Specific, Measurable, Aligned, Realistic, and Time-bound. These steps will help both of you mentally rehearse how the Plan will play out. Make sure to weave some positive reinforcement into the dialogue by expressing your Support, reassurance, and flexibility, and provide any other resources the coachee may need to become the owner of the Plan. The Plan that is created should be able to answer questions like the following:

- *What steps need to take place?*
- *Who will do what?*
- *Where will this take place?*
- *When will this happen?*
- *Using which resources?*
- *Measured against which standards?*

If there are many workable or practical courses of action available you may need to process your choices through a decision making procedure. There are many effective templates for decision-making, and most approaches are based on good common sense. We recommend the following process, as we have seen and experienced great results from using this approach:

1. Define the goals, results, or outcomes that you want to achieve as a result of the Plan, as well as the resources you have available to you.
2. Brainstorm and compare the options you've identified to the list of goals and resources you have.
3. Calculate how well each option is likely to perform against the goals you've set and the resources at your disposal.

Resist the temptation to jump at the first attractive option. Instead, look at your final choices carefully and assess whether they contain any potential obstacles, negative consequences, or undesirable side effects that could make the apparent number-one choice a bad option.

There are times when you must recognize and trust the strengths and differences that other people bring to the conversation. Creating a great Plan requires creative synergy. The goal is to maximize the power of two minds working together on a path forward.

Two Types of Plans

As you enroll people in the planning process, be aware that there are fundamentally two types of plans that can be created. The first type is the typical, forward-looking plan that helps produce change right away. This type of plan doesn't have to be complex. The level of detail present in the plan isn't overly critical at this point because the goal is simply to get some quick

action and forward momentum. Later, after things are set in motion, you can build on it or become more ambitious and elaborate with the plan. Starting small gives you and the person you are coaching a place to focus on, such as where you have a reasonable chance of capturing some early wins.

The second type of plan is one that focuses on issues that surface in the coaching process. For example, if you are still having differences of opinion and conflicts about the nature of the situation, you may need to create a Plan that aims to clarify the Impact or collect more data to validate the Topic. For example, you could help the people you are coaching create a plan to conduct a formal or informal survey, spend a few hours or days rotating jobs, take a temporary assignment with a different team, visit with a client, or something similar. In these situations, encourage your coaching partners to seek out the perspective of others, and be willing to do the same when it comes to getting outside of your own mental box. Ask them what plans or activities they can devise to help shed some new light on the situation and become better informed. These types of plans are expressly designed to help the parties gain insight about the Topic or Impact and ultimately produce a Plan with more substance.

Complex plans require the two coaching parties to invest some time, dig in deep, and do some research in order to design a rich, full solution. In other words, the "plan" is to get to a point where you can make a Plan! With either type of plan, you don't want to "fire" before you've taken careful aim at the right target and have enough valid information to make a smart move.

Recommendations for Planning Success

1. Begin the planning process with the desired outcome as your guiding light. A common goal for addressing the coaching Topic (not the personalities or egos of the two players) should be the primary driver in the coaching process.

2. Be cautious of devising one enormous master Plan aimed at solving a lot of big challenges and dilemmas all at once. Instead, start smaller and take "baby steps." Exercise a level of flexibility that is consistent with the situation and be willing to make alterations to the Plan along the way to ensure its success. A good Plan is one that is constructed with the idea that before you arrive at the final destination, some changes and modifications will be necessary. Make sure your coaching partner understands that you are willing and available to talk openly and make changes to the Plan as you move along the learning curve.

3. Sometimes it helps to share your understanding of the boundaries. We call this "chalking the field," which means helping to provide a framework of parameters or requirements to design a Plan within. In outdoor sports, the chalk lines simply inform players about the boundaries of play. In coaching discussions, you are essentially clarifying the goals, resources, talent, values, policies, and timelines that need to be considered as coachees choose a path, but also giving them flexibility in working within that space or field of play. Create an environment in which the other party has enough space to experiment and practice with new tools, behaviors, and processes.

4. Don't settle. Sometimes people are blindly determined to make a poor Plan work. Someone once told us that when you realize you're standing in a hole, you should stop digging; unfortunately, the tendency with a bad Plan often seems to be dig faster and try to force a positive outcome! Don't settle for a general concept or vague idea when something clear and precise is needed. It will save you time in the long run if the initial Plan you create is one that will move the project all the way through to completion.

5. As you devise a Plan, it's okay to encourage the coachee—and yourself—to stretch beyond perceived limits, as long as both parties feel supported as they take new risks. You can challenge others to push their limits until it begins to negatively affect their confidence. At that point, your job is to help others see the potential obstacles in the path and learn how best to work through them. Give your coachees the resources and moral support they need during the process.

6. Throughout the planning process, ask thought-provoking questions like the following:

   - *What is the situation trying to teach you that will be helpful in the future?*
   - *What are you learning?*
   - *When you encounter this situation again, what would you do differently?*
   - *What could you start or stop doing to achieve more of what you need?*
   - *How will you act or think in the future?*

These are strategic questions that work on the root issue while raising awareness and building a reflective-learning mindset.

7. Document the Plan. Remember that a good plan that has not been clearly outlined or documented is only a wish in your mind! It's essential that the Plan is solidified in a concrete way. Encourage coachees to post the plans they develop electronically or physically in their work space. This will act as a helpful reminder for them to take action and track their progress. Tracking the progress being made in a tangible way can also become a source of visual reinforcement. As a coach, you will also use the written Plan as a living document, something you can refer to during follow-up conversations. Having the Plan written down will help you hold coachees accountable if their motivation falters or they lose sight of the Impact of the issue at hand.

8. Perhaps the most important recommendation we can make in this chapter is to ask the coachee for a commitment to the agreement and plans that have been formulated. A clear acknowledgement of ownership is like a signature on a contract; we call it a verbal signature. Until you get that, you only have a concept or good idea. What you want is a firm, audible ownership of the Plan and commitment to seeing it through.

As we've said, when it comes to the "Plan" element of the Coaching TIPS² ™ Model, it is important to remember that a good solution requires more than a basic concept or series of actions. To make the Plan robust, you need to "seal the deal," and you do that by gaining a firm commitment. We often hear

stories of good plans failing because the parties involved didn't clearly articulate their commitment. Too many coaches conclude a conversation assuming that everyone is committed to the Plan when the ownership of it is actually far from clear. Without an unambiguous commitment, sustaining accountability becomes much more difficult.

This point was really driven home when one of the authors, Steve, was trying to gain closure on a marketing plan with one of our business-development colleagues. We will call him Don. After exploring the Plan in some detail, Steve asked Don this question: *"Do you think this plan is doable?"* Rather than responding to this simple yes/no question directly, Don redirected the conversation to the plan's timeline. At first, Steve didn't realize that Don was dodging the question (and avoiding making a clear commitment). Steve waited for a moment while Don made his point and then raised the question again. Once again, Don directed the discussion to a technicality about resources needed to execute the plan, which had already been discussed and dealt with just moments prior. At this point, Steve could tell Don's trepidation wasn't about resources or timing or anything else—it was about fear of accountability, fear of change, and fear of trying a marketing strategy that would take Don out of his comfort zone. It was clear that the only way to solidify the Plan and lock in the commitment was to boldly call out the resistance and get a candid answer. Finally, Steve said to Don, *"Let's step back for a minute. I've been trying to find out if you are all in on the plan, but you haven't answered my question. This plan is guaranteed to fail if it doesn't have your full commitment."* At that point, Steve simply stopped talking; he believes that silence can sometimes be the best communication tool. For a moment Don was quiet and contemplative.

It wasn't until Steve said, *"Don, on a scale of 1 to 10 with 10 meaning you support the plan completely, what is your number? I don't think it makes sense to work out more details until I understand your hesitation."* Don cautiously said, *"At this moment, I am at a 5."* Steve responded, *"That is exactly what I wanted to know. Let's figure out what it would take to get you more excited and engaged."* This experience really opened our eyes to how persistent you have to be when tying off on a Plan. Nothing can be accomplished until you have discovered what others are truly thinking and feeling about the go-forward plan of action.

In Summary

Tip #4: Plan is about creating "deliverables;" it is also about balancing both parties' level of involvement and their respective contributions. If you can focus on a common goal (the "end"), and if the other person is willing to help figure out the methods and tactics you will use to reach it (the "means"), you will create a powerful alliance. Ultimately, this will lead to a productive and stimulating long-term relationship that will continually change and improve over time. You are creating the opportunity for synergy, as well as for breakthroughs. You are setting the stage for ownership and greater interest and motivation for making needed improvements and changes a reality. Finally, you are reinforcing the idea that synergistic coaching is a consultative process that values input and uses it to help drive better action plans and establish the genuine commitment of coach and coachee alike.

CHAPTER

7

Tip #5: Sustain

"We are what we repeatedly do. Excellence,
then, is not an act, but a habit."

—Aristotle

In the Coaching TIPS²™ Model, "Sustain" refers to the per-severance needed to follow through with the coachee so you can achieve the goals that inspired you to engage in the two-way coaching experience in the first place. Some people mistakenly treat this tip as the ending point in the coaching process when it is actually better viewed as the *starting* point. If you subscribe to the notion that coaching is a process, not an event, you will see why this tip is really the beginning of the coaching journey.

In the Coaching TIPS²™ process, Tip #5: Sustain has a dual fo-cus: one concentrates on the short term, including the individual you are working with and the coaching Topic at hand; the other concentrates on the long term, including your commitment to building an enduring relationship. Your efforts will begin at the close of the coaching discussion as you lay the groundwork for how you will follow up, the ongoing coaching you will provide, and how you will help the coachee sustain action or change.

> *"After climbing a great hill, one only finds that*
> *there are many more hills to climb."*
> —**Nelson Mandela**

Let's explore what constitutes sustainability from five angles:

1. Discussing important outcomes and consequences
2. Being willing to accept some coaching yourself
3. Celebrating success
4. Ensuring accountability
5. Knowing when coaching isn't working

Discuss the Future Outcomes

As your coaching conversation begins to come to a close, look for an opportunity to clarify the outcomes and benefits that will result from achieving success with the changes you've identified. Also, be prepared to be candid and articulate the risks and potential exposure that will arise if the desired Plan and results don't materialize. We can't emphasize enough how important this is to the sustainability phase of the coaching process. This is where you can help the coachee think more deeply about the situation and ignite some excitement, as well as answering three questions that coachees will likely have in mind:

- *What's in it for me if we succeed?*
- *What's in it for all of us?*
- *What costs will we incur if the Plan is poorly executed?*

While the Impact tip attempts to ignite the *intrinsic* motivation, the Sustain tip is designed to spark the *extrinsic* motivation. When you unleash both, you create an unstoppable drive and people grow, evolve, and improve.

Over many years of studying the coaching process and observing people who coach in the workplace, we have noticed a disturbing trend: although it's possible to envision the positive or negative scenarios that are likely to unfold as a result of achieving (or conversely, *not* achieving) a Plan, managers rarely speak about them directly. In fact, after listening to over 1,000 recordings of coaching conversations, only 5% of the coaches were willing to wade into a discussion about the implications of a Plan's success or failure. When you link outcomes or consequences with behaviors, the coaching experience begins to click. That's what makes this part of the coaching process so important. People need to see that this change or Plan not only serves their personal interests, but also the interests of the team, the business, the customers, and other key stakeholders. Realizations like these help the conversation come to life and make the coaching personally meaningful to both parties. When people know what they can expect in terms of potential outcomes (positive or negative), they can align their actions accordingly. While the power of future-oriented consequences may be common knowledge and clear in the minds of many, openly discussing them is not common practice, nor are they clarified in the dialogue and interactions people have. You lose a lot of coaching's power when you fail to explore the scenarios that lie ahead.

What is often forgotten is that the goal of identifying consequences is to improve understanding and clarity, not to use this knowledge as some kind of punishment. Despite your best intentions, however, this component of coaching can occasionally be perceived as a harsh part of the process. Even though no one can perfectly predict what's to come, the coach is trying to help the coachee do a "reality check." When the people you are coaching are explicitly aware of potential outcomes, it garners additional interest and draws more attention to the Plan's implementation and/or sustained behavior change.

As the coachee works through the Plan, there may be times when his or her motivation will lag. If the coach has taken a positive and upbeat approach to identifying potential implications, the coachee will be able to pull additional motivation from focusing on the positive gains that could be achieved down the road. However, to be fair and avoid surprises, it's important for the coachee to understand both the positive and the negative possibilities, or the harm that could result from not executing the Plan of action. Keep in mind that negative consequences can be broached in a positive way if you so choose. Here are two examples:

- You could say, *"If we make the sale, here is how everyone wins,"* rather than saying, *"You know, if we don't get this sale, you won't hit your target for the year."*
- If your message to a team member is, *"If you don't follow these uniform safety practices, you risk losing your job,"* you could instead say, *"You know, when you and all of us support the safety regulations, it makes this a lot more secure and enjoyable place to work, and we reduce the risk of hurting people."*

Future outcomes come in two interesting forms. The first type is the "natural" variety. These consequences are the likely results of a particular course of action. Regardless of whether they are positive or negative, these consequences are largely governed by nature: if certain actions are followed, they should result in safe and productive activity. By the same token, if these governing ideas are *not* followed, the likely results are resistance, conflict, and pain. The second type of consequence is dictated by other people or the institutions they've constructed. In this case, the causes and effects are controlled by people and the power they have to reward or discipline others. For example, in a business, if a Plan does not meet the needs of the parties, the affected players may disengage or leave the team. On the other hand, if the Plan *does* meet the future needs of the coaching partners, you can expect to see greater levels of interest and enthusiasm.

As with any other part of a coaching discussion, identifying consequences should be a joint effort. Using questions like the following will help you draw out both the natural and imposed consequences during your discussion:

- *How do you see this Plan paying off?*
- *What are the risks that exist?*
- *How will a lack of success with the Plan prevent us from fulfilling our needs or achieving our vision?*

A coach should not get into the game of making promises; one simply has to look at the probability of various scenarios unfolding. This is how we offset the risks that either party may perceive in attempting to implement the solution, Plan, or agreement.

Be genuine when working to clarify consequences. You don't want to fabricate information or exaggerate the truth. Instead, try to figure out what it will actually take to Sustain the new effort, Plan, or agreement over time. As you anticipate the risks and rewards, clarify for the coachee that you are not interested in being insensitive or harsh, and that singling out or attacking the person is not your intention. Make sure your coaching partner knows that your goal with this discussion is to discover and understand the benefits and risks (or lack thereof) associated with the plan you've created.

If necessary, use this time in the coaching process to take one final look at the plan. If your associates aren't getting something back, if there isn't an interest in what you're trying to accomplish, or if there aren't any benefits to moving forward, the entire plan, agreement, or relationship may be in jeopardy.

Be Coachable

Before you conclude a coaching discussion, seek out some personal feedback (i.e. your behavior, your performance, and/ or the quality and effectiveness of the coaching process as you've been approaching it). Ask the person you are coaching to candidly tell you whether they are getting what they want and need from the relationship. See if the dialogue is working for them, and ask if they would like you to do anything differently the next time you interact with them in a coaching capacity. You don't need to make this feedback opportunity a big deal or solicit feedback in large quantities. You simply need to invite them to offer their honest opinions by asking a few basic questions:

- *How did this discussion work for you?*
- *Are you getting what you need?*
- *Am I doing enough to support your efforts?*
- *Was I too direct?*
- *Do you feel I have been clear?*
- *How can I help us forge a durable relationship?*

- *Has my agenda for this discussion been unclear or confusing in any way?*

Asking these types of questions and having open discussions about the effectiveness of your coaching approach will ensure that your intentions are clear and that you have demonstrated an active interest in being "coachable." The final suggestion we make is that you take the person's suggestions to heart. Most leaders want to be great coaches. They can be. We believe the best coaches are also "coachable," or willing to receive feedback from others and make adjustments as needed. Being coachable will help you grow as a person *and* make you a better coach.

In addition to inviting feedback, let your coaching partner know that you are committed to improving your skills and making a real contribution to the partnership. When people know that you are personally committed to the plan (and that they have your support as they work to make the change), you are more likely to see an increase in the coachee's dedication to moving the plan forward. However, in some cases, people will "test the waters" a bit by taking no action until they feel that they can trust you and have seen you fulfilling your responsibilities, as outlined in the plan. Your reliability and patience will be carefully scrutinized. As action begins to be taken on the plan, check your own levels of commitment, continue working on the action items you're responsible for in the plan, and then increase your communication with the coachee. This will help your coachees see and hear that you are fully committed to their growth, development, and success.

As you wrap up the initial coaching conversation, you should acknowledge the other person for the time, energy, and thought they have contributed to the discussion, express your optimism towards the plan, and assess their level of commitment one last time. If there are no concerns at that point, establish a date, place, and time for your next meeting. At a symbolic level, it may be beneficial to let the coachee pick the logistics of when and where to reconnect. If only one coaching partner consistently makes decisions about the follow-up process, it can lead to a perceived "home-court advantage." Nonetheless, this follow-up discussion can be held as soon as a few hours or a day or two after the initial coaching conversation, depending on the situation. However, keep in mind that without some reinforcement, plans and commitments will start to fade from consciousness after just a couple of days.

Celebrate Successes

"Celebrate what you want to see more of."
—Thomas J. Peters

Too often, people hold off on celebrating something until they arrive at their destination or end goal; interim achievements are rarely, if ever, acknowledged. One organization we worked with was unwilling to acknowledge the progress they were making towards success. They refused to celebrate their incremental achievements because they feared that members of the organization would relax their efforts at that point and assume they had "arrived." Tip #5: Sustain is based on a different mindset, one that is based on the belief that when incremental steps are celebrated, people will feel more motivated to carry on and push through. This tip serves as a reminder to celebrate the small wins towards the ultimate objective. Don't wait

until you have achieved perfection, because that rarely happens! Whenever possible, you and the coachee must find some joy in the journey.

> *"Perseverance is not a long race;*
> *it is many short races one after another."*
> —**Walter Elliott**

A key aspect of the Sustain element of the Model is its ability to help both parties mentally prepare to launch the initiative that has been planned. Some people have to experience a little success before they are able to positively believe in the change that is needed. In order to initiate and Sustain progress on the coaching Topic and Plan, you must try to help others *believe* they can win before they *see* the win.

As you coach and follow up, talk about and help the coachee visualize what progress and success will look and feel like. High-performance individuals envision progress and success in their minds before they start the work. This is a vital part of the coaching process. A successful track-and-field high jumper, Dwight Stones, would close his eyes and mentally experience the jump long before he would take the first step toward the cross-bar. You could visibly see him move his head, shoulders, and the rest of his body as he rehearsed his approach. Michael Jordan, the famous basketball player, did the same thing before he shot each free throw. Your coachee may find this visualization process helpful as well, so encourage them to engage in positive mental images and internal dialogue as they execute the plan. We like to call this "self-coaching." In life, you can practice these tips in many situations where you become your own best coach.

The Accountability Factor

Ensuring accountability is another important ingredient of the Coaching TIPS²™ Model. After the initial coaching discussion(s), it is critical to have follow-up discussions or touch points where you can monitor progress, offer help, and work through any problems or challenges. We like to refer to them as "touch and go's." Remember, the purpose of following up with your coachee is not to smother or micromanage their efforts. Rather, you are trying to demonstrate your commitment to helping them achieve a successful outcome and complete what you set out to do. This ongoing contact serves two purposes:

1. Enables you to support, revise, and recommit to the Plan on a regular basis.
2. Ensures that the trusting relationship you built with your coachee stays strong after the initial coaching discussion.

The need to follow up and ensure accountability can't be overemphasized because it is what ultimately allows you to close the loop on the coaching Topic. And don't worry: it's virtually impossible to guide, teach, or follow up with the coachee too much when you're striving to build a synergistic relationship.

Your goals for follow-up discussions are to ensure, in a positive and supportive way, that the commitments you've made are honorable and that your agreements have integrity.

Most of us would like to see the change process start fast, kicked immediately into "high gear." We have said repeatedly that coaching requires patience, and so it is with this element of the Model. Give the person a chance to get the Plan launched and headed in the right direction. In some situations, you may have to accept some false starts as the Plan gets up and running. Each follow-up encounter certainly doesn't merit a full-blown coaching conversation, but it is important to be very transparent and communicative with the coachee about your resolve to move forward. Your goals for follow-up discussions are to ensure, in a positive and supportive way, that the commitments you've made are honorable and that your agreements have integrity. These follow-up opportunities are an ideal time to restore your commitment to the process and to the other person. If, in these discussions, you find that commitment is low and there has been a lack of success or follow-through, it may be time to develop new ideas, action plans, and strategies and obtain a fresh commitment to the new plans you generate.

> However, if you discover during your follow-up discussions that there has been less success than you would have expected, don't panic.

The first signs of visible action are critical because they provide tangible proof of the coachee's level of ownership for the Plan and desired outcomes. However, if you discover during your follow-up discussions that there has been less success than you would have expected, don't panic. Begin by retracing your steps through the Coaching TIPS²™ Model and use it to pinpoint where the follow-through might be breaking down. Verify that the real issue is being addressed, not just its symptoms. As you do so, show Support for the person. You want to express to the other person, in no uncertain terms, that the coaching dialogue and contact will end ONLY if the coachee chooses to stop the process. Take time to communicate to the coachee your determination to get things moving again and your enthusiasm

You want to express to the other person, in no uncertain terms, that the coaching dialogue and contact will end ONLY if the coachee chooses to stop the process.

for the process. Continue working with your coachees for as long as they are making an effort. Don't give up on them! And don't give up on the Coaching TIPS²™ Model, either. Even if it doesn't seem to be working (right away), you must be patient and learn to trust the coaching process. Each coaching opportunity will feel different. It never goes perfectly, so prepare yourself for some up and downs along the way.

> *"Success seems to be largely a matter of hanging on after others have let go."*
> —**William Feather**

When Coaching Doesn't Work

We often get asked, *"Are there times when you should give up?"* You must keep in mind that behavior change is usually *evolutionary*, not *revolutionary*. Deep and important change rarely occurs overnight, which makes sustaining your coaching efforts all the more critical. You cannot force change, or the coaching process, onto others. We recognize that there are some cases where the coaching process just isn't the right "fit." If you have a situation where coaching isn't working, don't work yourself into a self-defeating cycle by trying to make the coaching process work when it can't. Sometimes people are defiant and balk at being coached, but neither the process nor the situation is at fault. Remain loyal and dedicated to the coaching principles and skills, but know that generally, if you're still having no luck after three good-faith efforts with an individual, you can acknowledge that the situation may not be right for the coaching process.

Every once in a while, you will encounter extreme cases where people simply aren't interested in growth, learning, collaboration, or even teamwork. Some people get stuck in self-destructive patterns and may even

If you're still having no luck after three good-faith efforts with an individual, you can acknowledge that the situation may not be right for the coaching process.

require professional help to move forward in a healthy way. However, studies have found that people who are determined not to support the change, the organization, or themselves can only be helped in limited ways, even with professional intervention. The spirit of the message is this: don't give up too soon. Be aware that in a learning environment, both partners must be willing to live with some false starts, pushback, or normal resistance. When this does occur, take the personality of the coachee into consideration. Remember that some people prefer to be given a little space as they regroup. Give them the space they need, build up their confidence and determination, and try again. Other people will prefer you to immediately step in and help them buoy their spirits. Some people thrive on reinforcement and recognition and some don't. What you can do is remind them of the potential positive outcomes of reaching the goal. You may also decide that it's a good idea for the two of you to conduct a review of the Plan, and when needed, break it down even further and identify some new "baby steps" to get you started in the right direction again.

Some Final Thoughts

"With ordinary talent and extraordinary perseverance,
all things are attainable."
—Thomas Foxwell Buxton

Coaching others is a lot like driving a car: even after a direction has been determined and the journey has begun, midcourse changes may be needed. Mileposts suggest the driver may be off course or off schedule. Small or large adjustments may need to be made to stay on course or get back on course. These adjustments and changes come in the form of actions taken by the coach that are designed to support and sustain the change process. Sometimes the driver, or coachee, adjusts direction by nudging the steering wheel. Other times, the coachee may turn the car around, take a new route, or alter the final destination. Resist the urge to grab the wheel and take control. Remember that your job as a coach is to help your coachees navigate through the process and support them through the detours and obstacles in the journey and beyond.

> You don't have to be perfect at working the coaching process. You must simply become good at using it—by being consistent and disciplined.

You don't have to be *perfect* at working the coaching process. You must simply become *good* at using it—by being consistent and disciplined.

CHAPTER

8

Interference, Challenges, Obstacles, & Resistance

"Obstacles are those frightful things you see when you take your eyes off your goal."

—Henry Ford

Invariably, whenever new behaviors, plans, or solutions of any kind are implemented, there are bound to be some headwinds or opposing forces that can get in the way. This is often true when coaching others. Coaching obstacles can come in the form of challenges that come from the environment; they can also manifest as other types of interference such as struggling to gain support and cooperation from others or find the resources needed to implement a Plan of action. These are considered "hard" obstacles and challenges. Interestingly, the more daunting problems are often the "soft" challenges: the internal obstacles and battles people face. Although these behaviors and situations can be uncomfortable and difficult to work through for both parties, it is important to remember that resistance

Resistance and pushback are a natural part of growth and change. The coaching process itself will help you work through these behaviors effectively.

to change is a normal human reaction. When these responses begin to surface, they are a signal to you as the coach that the other person may be experiencing some fear, anxiety, and/or frustration in response to the coaching process in general or the Plan in particular. Resistance and pushback are a natural part of growth and change. The coaching process itself will help you work through these behaviors effectively. In this chapter, you will learn more about the coaching obstacles, challenges, and common signs of resistance and how to recognize them. You will also learn how to address different types of objections and excuses, which signs of resistance are most common, and how to stay focused on your coaching goals when interference and challenges arise. As you read, keep in mind that helping others work through impediments can be empowering and rewarding for both parties.

In the Coaching TIPS²™ Model, the element "Interference, Challenges, Obstacles, & Resistance" is not depicted in the same way as the other tips. Rather, this circular element touches each of the tips and appears faintly behind all of them. It isn't a numbered step of the Model because these behaviors can appear and become a distraction at any stage during a coaching conversation, and later when action is being taken. Occasionally, some conversations will be entirely devoid of interference and resistance, but this is rare. This tends to happen when someone feels a need to change direction and is willing to take action on their own, without requiring much outside influence from the coach.

Why Interference, Challenges, Obstacles, & Resistance?

Whenever we embark on a new journey, there are always going to be some inherent risks and/or challenges. The greatest cause of resistance is the anticipation and fear of these potential risks and problems. Denial, fighting against change, and coming up with excuses are very common reactions to uncomfortable realities. They stem from a person's fear or anxiety about moving into a new place or heading in a new direction. It's a lot like climbing a ladder: every step that a person takes up the ladder goes against the pull of gravity and each step can be a little scarier than the last. Fear and discomfort pull against progress in a similar way. The "new or different" can be viewed as frightening and more painful than the existing situation. The status quo is familiar and feels safe, even if the coachee recognizes that the current situation is ineffective or won't work in the long run. People will often acknowledge that the Plan is *possible*, but they may not feel entirely motivated to move in a new direction due to mixed emotions or insecurity related to making the change. That is the moment when ambivalence sets in: *"I want to, but I don't want to"* (or, *"yes, but..."*).

Though it may be disheartening and frustrating, the presence of resistant behaviors and excuses can actually be helpful. Excuses can be a signal to the coach about whether the coachee understands the Impact of the situation, feels supported, believes the Plan is possible, and has made an honest commitment to making a change. In fact, resistance and excuses most commonly appear

By successfully working through resistance that occurs in the form of excuses, you can increase the level of trust in the relationship, create tighter plans, and strengthen commitment.

when a coach asks for the coachee's verbal commitment to the Plan in Tip #4 of the Model. By successfully working through resistance that occurs in the form of excuses, you can increase the level of trust in the relationship, create tighter plans, and strengthen commitment. However, if they are left unaddressed, defensiveness can set in and change can be harder to achieve.

The Courage to Confront

Similar to the other parts of the Coaching TIPS[2™] Model, addressing obstacles and resistance requires a little courage and perceptiveness by the coach. It takes a stout heart to engage your coaching partner, state your observations about resistance or obstacles, and guide them through the coping process. Even the coach needs to be prepared to acknowledge their own resistance. Negativity, pessimism, and cynicism present a formidable challenge—one that you must be prepared to confront. It's also important to remember that resistance is a double-edged sword: both the coach and the coachee are likely to dig their heels in at certain points during the coaching process, and both partners are capable of resisting each other's ideas, suggestions, and potential changes.

Adults like their autonomy and freedom. When a coach ignores this fact, the coachee's determination to further defy change and rational thought is amplified. A coaching opportunity can be turned into a stalemate if it's approached in the wrong way.

You may have noticed that we use the term "confront" when it comes to addressing Interference, Challenges, Obstacles, & Resistance. While the word "confront" may initially feel a bit aggressive to you, it underscores the fact that a coach must be honest and courageous in bringing the detrimental—and potentially, disastrous—effects of resistance to the forefront of the conversation. Resistance needs to be openly addressed so solutions can be explored. Please understand that this element is *not* a platform for either coaching partner to argue with the other or to create a conflict; engaging in either behavior will only solidify the resistance.

The Positive Side

When a coach redirects the conversation and helps the other person stay focused on actions rather than obstacles and excuses, many benefits can be gained:

- Provides an opportunity for the coach to be proactive and address barriers and excuses that identify the coachee's concerns or bring potential problems to light.
- Builds and maintains a positive foundation for solving problems.
- Works through interpersonal issues (like trust) and supports open communication.
- Identifies and deals with obstacles or feelings that may impede the creation of a productive relationship.
- Keeps the discussion focused and solution-oriented.
- Helps the coachee manage and cope with the uncomfortable and often-harsh realities of change.

Achieving ultimate success with coaching depends on your ability to anticipate the resistance and to have the courage to name it or call it out. However, the courage to be candid must be balanced with sensitivity so your coaching partner won't feel threatened by your approach.

In Los Angeles County, traffic cops can expect to get at least a few complaints documented in their personnel file every year, most of which are trivial complaints from people who are upset because they got a ticket and it ruined their day or those who are in denial about their actions. Captain Patrick Maxwell was shocked when he discovered that one of his Sheriff Deputies, Elton Simmons, did not have a single complaint in 20 years with over 25,000 traffic stops. You read that right—he hadn't received a single complaint! So how does he do it? According to the Los Angeles Times' report on Simmons' accomplishment, "…he lives by the motto instilled in him by an uncle, who was a pastor, back home in Louisiana: 'Do good, be good, treat people good.'" When Simmons first moved to California, he says he was pulled over often and was uncomfortable with the animosity that was prevalent in those situations. He vowed to take a different approach when he became a police officer. In a story by CBS News, they observed that "Simmons' warm, friendly demeanor keeps citizens on his good side." Instead of saying things like, "Do you know how fast you were going?" or "Do you know why I've pulled you over?" Simmons takes a different approach and says things like, "Good morning, how are you?" or "The reason I'm stopping you today is because…" and then shows them the clock on the laser gun to avoid any potential denial. Coaches can learn a lot from Sheriff Elton Simmons about the importance of behaving in a supportive way when bringing a problem to light—especially problems or opportunities that have the potential to be met with denial, excuses, resistance or, in Sheriff Simmons' case, complaints. Don't underestimate the power that can come from being a supportive coach.

Excuses

Excuses are the most common (and for many coaches, the peskiest) obstacles coaches will encounter. When excuses are present, it is a signal to you that you are confronting some potential resistance. This section will help you understand at a deeper level the excuses that come your way and how to assess the meaning of each excuse; you will also learn how to address them in an appropriate way, and without sidetracking the conversation.

A smart coach knows that in every coaching opportunity, excuses may materialize and block the progress of the conversation and the Plan. Working through this is a little bit like making headway in a volleyball game: when the Plan is being "spiked" by excuses or resistance and placed at risk, you need to "dig" and make extra effort to keep the ball in play. With coaching, this doesn't mean you can ignore or attack—it just means you need to strategize a rational prevention and contingency plan.

The Two Types of Excuses

Every excuse made can fall into one of two categorizes: "Type I" or "Type II." According to our definitions, a Type I excuse prevents the two parties from discussing the Topic or issue in a meaningful way and restricts accurate data from being gathered. Type I excuses are usually rooted in past events and are typically harmless, although sometimes they can be bothersome.

Type II excuses, on the other hand, prevent the parties from moving forward and can paralyze the coaching process. We will describe each type in more detail below and provide examples so you will be able to discern which type of excuse you're

encountering while you coach. This will also help you understand how best to help the coachee work through it.

Type I Excuses

Type I excuses typically show up when you focus on the
coaching Topic, need, or Impact of the situation and the coachee
wants to minimize or shift responsibility away from this sensitive
Topic or discussion. Type I excuses help individuals tolerate the
raw nerve of current reality and feel better about the status quo.
They attempt to make their current approach, choices, or behavior seem acceptable and in alignment with expectations and
standards by pulling those standards down to a lower level.

A lot of Type I excuses indicate that Impact hasn't been
properly established. An Impact void leads to more denial and
allows defensiveness and resistance to fill in the gap. These
Type I excuses can be recognized by simply identifying the
time frame of the excuse. If your coaching partner is resisting
the Topic by citing events and circumstances that have already
occurred, you are likely experiencing a classic Type I excuse.
When someone feels threatened (or when they perceive that
others are not listening to their side of the story), they try to
over-explain their situation or history to prove their point. Furthermore, they may use events that are outside of their individual control or sphere of influence to justify themselves and their
behavior—and to protect their self-esteem.

Running into repetitive Type I excuses can feel like a yo-yo
effect. Exposing the Topic or Impact will often cause defensive
reactions, even if the coaching opportunity does not suggest
intentional misbehavior. The Topic may inadvertently suggest
to the coachee that he or she has committed an error by not
recognizing a new opportunity. The coachee's "not invented

here" mentality begins to breed its own unique form of resistance; that is, *"If I don't see the Topic first or invent the solution, I won't support it."*

The more you present the coaching Topic as a constructive, positive opportunity and look at the glass as being "half full," the less likely you are to get bogged down by Type I excuses. For example, if you position the Topic by saying, *"Why didn't you get the assignment done in time?"* you are virtually guaranteed to be inundated with Type I excuses of all kinds. However, if you say, *"Will you help me figure out ways to decrease the turnaround time on certain assignments and projects?"* instead, you are less likely to snag a Type I excuse simply because it doesn't feel like a personal attack or accusation. When you say, *"Will you help me figure out how to enhance customer service?"* or *"How can we drive out more cost or increase sales?"* the Topic is on neutral or positive ground. If there is a problem, then make the causes of this problem a subset of the Topic and explore them in a very matter-of-fact and non-aggressive manner. For example, you might say, *"Will you give me your opinion about the reasons for the accident rate increasing? I am deeply concerned about this."*

Type II Excuses

Type II excuses come from obstacles (real or imagined) that are perceived to prevent the agreement or Plan from being carried out; they inhibit movement or action related to the coaching from taking place. Type II excuses are more substantive. They are worth learning about and exploring in detail. We say these excuses originate "upstream" because they are insights and clues about events that are flowing your way. These excuses will be created or focused on to the degree that agreement and commitment is difficult or even painful to achieve. A research study by M.R. Leary and J.A. Shepperd describe "self-hand-icap" as "a verbal claim that a personal weakness or problem limits their control on the performance of a task. This creates a sense in one's mind that underperforming could not be helped." When the self-handicap is directed towards a current or future Plan or agreement, individuals are trying to control the perceptions and beliefs that others have of them. If a person sets up a Type II excuse (such as claiming to be sick) the day before a big assignment or test and their subsequent performance isn't as strong as he or she had hoped, the poor performance can be rationalized and the person can avoid personal responsibility. The "self-handicap" (in this case, illness) lowers expectations and creates a mechanism for dodging accountability. Even perceived (imagined) constraints and novel resistance require you to work constructively and reframe your mindset or vision to focus on success with the Plan rather than the barriers that will prevent it from being carried out. Again, you'll need to be patient and supportive as the coach. In high-stress situations, the most effective coaching technique may simply be to allow your partners to vent their feelings and concerns.

Sometimes Type II excuses can be recognized by their relationship to catharsis. By allowing your coaching partner to vent these feelings, frustrations, concerns, etc., you may even see your partner come full circle back to the Impact of the coaching Topic after the Type II excuse has been aired. The coachee may recognize that the real or perceived obstructions need him or her to make an active effort in order to progress or move forward.

To a great extent, Type II excuses provide valuable insights into a person's level of commitment, the thinking process, and potential obstacles. These insights provide feedback on how effectively and rapidly the coaching process is working. You may not be able to completely prevent or eliminate all Type II excuses, but you can adopt a proactive stance, even at a token or symbolic level, to help mount a response to the obstacle of concern. Think of Type II excuses as resources or opportunities.

Understanding the underlying nature of Type II excuses gives you a new appreciation for their value. They are the first sign that the Plan may need adjustment, and that more patience, preparation, and thinking will be required if progress is to be made. On a positive note, they also mean that the coachee is invested, engaged, and trying to figure out how to make the Plan work. As a coach, you need to channel their thinking towards being solution-focused rather than obstacle-focused. If you approach coachees with the mindset of providing growth opportunities rather than seeing the situation as problematic, you will have greater success helping them deal with obstacles that stand in the way of their growth and development. This approach sets the foundation for no-fault coaching. No-fault coaching focuses on the process or procedure, not the person's character.

Sources of Excuses

Excuses come in many forms. They are often very creative, and sometimes they are legitimate. Listed below are some of the more specific and common types of excuses that you may encounter while coaching.

Institutional Beliefs

These excuses focus on big, uncontrollable things such as the government, the economy, laws, the older/younger generations, top management, investors, and customers. These can be very effective obstacles to accomplishment because a single individual can have very little impact on these things. As a result, they are convenient avenues for people to attempt to escape responsibility for being accountable or taking action.

People

Blaming others for shortcomings, mistakes, or lack of action is a convenient excuse. For example, claiming that renewed efforts and plans will be effective only when others cooperate is an excellent excuse. People often say, *"If only I could get others to cooperate, we could really move forward,"* or *"I can't predict how someone is going to respond to this new idea."* Acting helpless and positioning oneself as at the mercy of others (peers, leaders, suppliers, customers, and so forth) is really easy to do. The truth is, people can't be controlled but they *can* be influenced in a positive way. You can also develop processes that will help offset what others do to interfere with the Plan.

Denial

Denial takes many forms: arguing, hostility, interrupting, disagreeing, ignoring, silence, or excessive agreeableness. How you respond to your partner's simple denial behaviors makes a difference and is a true test of your supportiveness as a coach. Synergistic coaching will help you and your partner come to terms with these difficult obstacles.

Fears and Habits

Some people feel like they can't move forward because they did not come up with the idea; others believe they are unable to progress with the Plan because certain habits or comforts restrict them from trying new ideas. They may also fear negative repercussions. Many people allow their own memory to be the scapegoat—after all, "forgetting" is an innocent way to avoid responsibility. It doesn't require a decision, it just happens, and we can't be expected to remember everything. After all, we're only human. As with all excuses, when confronting people's fears and habits, understanding needs to be combined with resourceful thinking to counterbalance the challenge.

Time

Clock and calendar excuses deal with the fact that people are just too busy and don't seem to have time for everything they're asked to do. When time excuses crop up, it is usually because people are caught in a reactionary activity trap. It is difficult to distinguish *urgent* activities from *important* activities. Consequently, people easily fall into a vicious cycle of always having to "put out fires." Some feel that they just can't fit one more thing into their already overly full schedules; others are simply unwilling to drop old strategies or old paradigms that currently occupy their calendars and keep them from doing new or difficult things.

Information

How many times have you said, *"I didn't know…"*? Maybe you assert, to the kind officer of the law, that you didn't know the speed limit was so low in this part of town. Or maybe you're absolutely certain that you never received the email or message or heard the announcement. An excuse about having a lack of information can be very hard to deal with because the only person who knows for sure if the excuse is true is the person making the claim.

Environment

Sometimes people will use environmental factors as an excuse. In addition, road conditions, traffic, construction, accidents, supplies, material defects, etc., can be used as distractions from the real issue. It is important to remember, and to remind others, that obstacles and headwinds will always exist. There will always be unexpected inconveniences that can interfere with your work. As a coach, you need to help others understand that they need to prepare for some obstacles, headwinds, and delays. Navigating through these kinds of inconveniences or disruptions is simply part of our complex and fast-paced world—and part of the development process.

Saving Face

The coachee may also use excuses to preserve his or her image so the coach will retain a more favorable impression. In the medical community, two separate studies have shown that patients will often complain about physical symptoms to cover up psychological or relationship problems. In fact, doctors estimate that two-thirds of their time is spent treating individuals whose real problems aren't actually physiological. What is critical in coaching is to remember that people may deflect issues onto something else or make other complaints. When this happens, they are not necessarily being deceitful; rather, they may be using adverse circumstances as an excuse but may not even realize that they're doing so. Coaching becomes more challenging when your partners take a valid excuse or complaint and try to leverage it too much, seek to gain sympathy or attention, or try to guard against negative impressions that others might form.

Response Options

When excuses crop up in your conversations, you have a great opportunity to further apply the Coaching TIPS² ™ Model.

Even if you only provide the coachee with a little bit of help to manage his or her justifications, it can keep things on a more positive and constructive plane. Before you read further and learn more about how to respond to excuses, we'd like to suggest that you don't spend too much time and effort sorting out whether the excuses are legitimate or not. Regardless of the validity of the excuse, you'll typi-

> **Don't spend too much time and effort sorting out whether the excuses are legitimate or not.**

cally handle it in the same authentic and legitimate way. Additionally, if your coaching partners pick up on the idea that you think their excuses are artificial, their defensiveness will kick in, even if they know that the excuse isn't genuine.

1. Stay On Alert

The first key to confronting Interference, Challenges, Obstacles, & Resistance head on is to avoid letting these behaviors catch you off guard. While unforeseen events will surprise you at times, highly effective coaches make a strong effort to stay consciously aware of any signs that may indicate the presence of resistance to the coaching process. Take a proactive, rather than a reactive, approach to spotting resistance whenever possible. Reacting to resistance and excuses may require you to retrace your steps from the beginning of the conversation, which can be a lot of work. However, when necessary, that is the beauty of the Model: it is a fluid process.

While excuses are fairly easy to recognize, other resistant behaviors may not be as obvious. For example, some people mistake resistance for healthy debate when, in fact, it almost always leads to obstacles to reaching an agreement and accepting responsibility. There are a few simple questions you can mull over while coaching that will help you spot resistance:

- *Does this person overanalyze the Plan?*
- *Does this person typically make excuses?*
- *Does this person seem unusually quiet or unresponsive?*
- *Does this person appear overly agreeable?*
- *Does this person seem upset or angry?*
- *Does this person change the subject?*
- *Does this person argue or debate the minute details of the Topic?*
- *Does this person seem focused on the past?*
- *Does this person postpone or delay taking the first step?*

Again, resistance is a common reaction to attempting something new, big, or challenging. Coaches plan on it; they anticipate it and figure out how to move through it without letting it stop the momentum.

2. Name the Excuse

One particularly effective approach to dealing with excuses is to "name it" in objective and descriptive terms. This is the act of acknowledging the resistant behavior and *temporarily* making it the Topic of the coaching discussion. Metaphorically speaking, you hold up a mirror and allow the coachee to observe his or her own behavior. For example, you might say, *"I can't help but notice that you seem to be focusing on the reasons why this Plan won't work."* Like we've stated before, keep your description of or observations about the situation brief. Use descriptive language that is clear and assertive but does not suggest an inference or judgment about the character of the other person. Make a statement about what the coachee is doing; don't frame your observation as a question. Asking a question calls for them to defend themselves, while a statement—posed in neutral and descriptive terms and followed by silence—calls for them to interpret or reflect on their behavior. Coaching partners may recognize the resistance for themselves if it's pointed out in a constructive way. Be prepared to offer Support so the coachee can avoid feeling overly exposed. If they respond with denial, which typically means that your observations are on target, be ready to start the process of re-direction. Coaches who are quick to discount the effectiveness of the "naming" method are likely feeling nervous about trying this method or awkward when using it. Believe us when we say that this method, when used in conjunction with the Coaching TIPS² ™ Model, has been highly effective and widely utilized by successful coaches. In fact, business guru Peter Block recommends this approach when consulting with and advising others.

Coaches who are quick to discount the effectiveness of the "naming" method are likely feeling nervous about trying this method or awkward when using it. Believe us when we say that this method, when used in conjunction with the Coaching TIPS²™ Model, has been highly effective and widely utilized by successful coaches.

3. Use Support

As you and the other person begin to deal with the re-sistance or obstacles that are blocking your path to success, don't lose sight of the Support element of coaching. Handling excuses and resistance respectfully by increasing the level of Support you're giving to the coachee can sometimes have a surprising effect: commitment to the Plan will grow naturally and resistance to it will die a natural death. Unfortunately, some coaches don't use Support enough and take a more aggressive approach, either "putting down" the excuse or trying to use their power and authority to discredit the validity of the excuse. You might see this tactic in statements such as, *"I think that is a ridiculous point."* Unsurprisingly, this approach is rarely effective and is inconsistent with the beliefs underlying partnership coaching. It creates a "vertical" or hierarchical relationship, as well as resentment and unresolved negative feelings. Similarly, arguing and debating with the other person on the logic and benefits of implementing the Plan or trying to coerce the coachee into accepting the coaching Topic can be harmful to the process. One example of arguing would be, *"But let me point out for the third time that, in an article I saw on the Internet, it said we should do it this way..."* This debate-style approach to communication is overused and can become unnecessarily manipulative. Alternatively, expressing some Support and showing some respect and empathy creates the conditions for a more productive dialogue.

If you are proactively looking for signs of Interference, Challenges, Obstacles, & Resistance, it's likely that you're already showing Support by being attentive, listening carefully, and remaining present in the discussion. However, when resistance begins to surface, conduct a mental check to make sure that your rapport with the other person hasn't diminished and that you're still clearly providing your Support.

4. Use Silence

When dealing with difficult behaviors, selective silence is a vastly underutilized method of communication and a powerful coaching tool. Not only does it demonstrate your willingness to let the other person speak, but a little silence after you have pointed out the resistance will give the coachee ample time to reflect on your observations and information, as well as to re-think or process their own thoughts.

5. Explore the Avoidance

Avoidance is often the result of the fear and hesitation that comes from dealing with the unknown. Some people can easily become consumed with the fear of failure rather than focus-ing on the possibility of success. This irrational preoccupation represents common avoidance behavior that many people expe-rience. For example, when you go to the doctor, when you an-ticipate the complexities of taking the test to renew your driver's license, or if you determine it will be better in the long run to change careers, you may experience a wide range of reactions: anything from *"let's get going"* to *"no way."* It is not unusual to anticipate the worst-case scenario; the cycle of avoidance can go on and on, as there is no limit to your imagination. You can dig a hole for yourself that is impossible to get out of, and most of this "hole" exists only in your own mind. Dr. Robin Kowalski at Western Carolina University conducted a study on complaints and excuses and learned that some are authentic, and some are not. Authentic complaints are usually due to real feelings of dis-satisfaction, whereas inauthentic complaints are not. In these cases, the excuse is driven by a desire to gain sympathy or assis-tance, or it can be a type of manipulation. As a coach, your role is to help the person you are coaching see the positive scenarios and move past the reservations they are feeling.

6. Ignore It

One of the quickest methods of addressing an excuse is to not address it at all! There will be occasions when an excuse you hear from a coachee is so outlandish that it is best to simply listen to it—and then ignore it. After all, the coachee may simply be giving you cues indicating their fears about moving forward and may know that the excuse isn't actually legitimate. Don't give it any more attention than it deserves.

7. Respond and Redirect

Those skilled in martial arts understand the concept of using the energy of the other person to help in their own self-defense. Even though coaching doesn't always involve a conflict, so to speak, another person's energy can still be used to effectively combat resistance. If people have the energy to think of excuses, they probably have the energy to begin working on some solutions. While ignoring an excuse is always an option, the excuses or obstacles the coachee throws your way (whether they're legitimate or not) usually require some kind of response from you. What matters is that you communicate to the other person that you hear what he or she is saying, but interferences, challenges, excuses, and resistance can't stand in the way of progress. As you work through excuses with the coachee, actively listen to and consider his or her perspective. This will help you understand what he or she is actually trying to say and the root cause of the resistance. Offer reassurance and test your interpretation of the excuses by summarizing and restating the excuses back to the coachee.

When it looks as if you are headed towards an impasse, clarify that your intention is to not say the other person is wrong. Indicate that you see the issue and understand their reservations, but you believe that different possibilities and solutions exist and you would like to explore them. Explain that you simply have a different take on the situation. It is okay to respectfully disagree and still keep the coaching process moving. Your goal is to provide tactful dialogue and leadership—and then *inquire* as much as you *advocate* for a particular position. Try to gently and subtly redirect the excuses you hear towards taking some small, constructive actions; encourage the coachee to respond to and think about the situation in a more pos-

When it looks as if you are headed towards an impasse, clarify that your intention is to not say the other person is wrong, but you believe that different possibilities exist and you would like to explore them.

itive, forward-thinking way. For example, you might say, *"You have a good point. This won't work unless we incorporate some kind of training to go along with our Plan. What are your ideas on how the training can be accomplished?"* Redirecting gets the notion across that both parties must accept the challenge of managing the obstacles to taking action. Explore whether constructive and substantive actions can be taken to prevent further potential problems, or if contingency or backup plans will minimize the overall potential Impact of adverse events that could come to pass.

8. Confront Your Own Resistance

As we mentioned earlier in this chapter, resistance can stem from both parties. As a coach, you must be prepared to face your own resistance, hesitations, and fears about trying new ideas or moving forward into uncharted waters. Be open to receiving help from others in working through your own ideas and developing creative new solutions. If, as coach, you can learn to think through possible scenarios yourself, you can also help others learn to envision the "what-if's" and think through them in a constructive way. If you look at excuses or resistance as a valuable element of the coaching dialogue, you will begin to feel less frustrated when excuses arise. And if you can identify, bring to the surface, and work through your own excuses and resistance, it will be easier for your coaching partners to do the same.

A Word of Caution

Problems will arise if you overuse some approaches or discuss the situation for too long or too intensely. It is possible for tension to develop if you try to oversell your perspective or ignore the other person's point or pain. You may get into an unrelenting rut, and the other person may begin to resist you and your methods more than the issue or excuse that you are trying to address! You can't expect to see automatic or immediate results of your efforts with any of these approaches. It will take some time for your chosen method to work, for the message to sink in, and for trust to develop. Don't rush it. The fruits of your labor will mature over time.

What If Resistance Continues?

Resistance is either a reaction to a set of circumstances or a choice that is being made, either consciously or subconsciously, by the other person. Even with all of your good-faith efforts, there is no "magic bullet" that will cut through resistance. Make two or three good-faith efforts to confront the resistance and shine a light on the situation but recognize that the person may become entrenched in their perspective or resistant stance if you continue to push. When you are trapped in a cycle of resistance, there are two approaches that you can take. First, objectively clarify the consequences of failing to change or successfully implement the Plan. Vividly illustrating the possible outcomes may shift the conversation and get it onto a productive course. As you may recall, we discussed how to identify natural and imposed consequences in detail in Chapter 7, "Tip #5: Sustain." Ultimately, resistance and excuses can become the greatest barrier to a coach, especially when resistance and excuses override the original Topic you wanted to explore.

The second approach can be employed if you recognize that this situation does not lend itself to a straightforward coaching conversation. In these more complex cases, you may want to seek out a third party—an advisor or mentor the coachee is comfortable with—to help or encourage the coachee to see the other side of the issue. Above all, don't quit. These alternatives may be the only help you can provide, and although this new Plan may be different or smaller than initially expected, it will be a Plan nonetheless. The coaching approach teaches the principle of never giving up. This principle focuses on persistence and the need to help the partnership maintain a positive vision of moving forward, even if the movement is accomplished through incremental, symbolic steps. You may not achieve all the plans, agreements, and changes that you want, but you can move forward by taking a few first steps and building from there.

In Summary

John Paul Jones is a strong example of a leader who had great determination. His ship was burning in a naval encounter during the American Revolutionary War. When he was asked if he would surrender, his famous response was, *"I have not yet begun to fight!"* But remember, the fight is not with the person who demonstrates resistance—the fight is to be relentless in the pursuit of solutions. If you can help instill a little bit of John Paul Jones' spirit and encourage others to continue with their efforts, despite the challenges that may come, you are truly living the coaching process. In fact, that is exactly the mindset that synergistic coaching is trying to inspire: life is all about putting forth great effort and overcoming obstacles so you can reach the top.

CHAPTER
9

Coaching Outcomes

Because coaching is an investment that requires time, energy, talents, and resources from the coach and coachee, performance coaching should provide returns that will benefit everybody involved—not only the individual, but the team and the entire organization. As a result of your efforts to coach individuals and groups, you will see an improvement in your bottom line. Our research has shown that companies can achieve a 5% increase in bottom-line performance when they actively coach others. Countless other studies and research projects conducted on coaching in a variety of working environments have found similar results. In addition to the economic gains that can come from coaching, there is a range of other important outcomes that are worth aiming for during the coaching journey, all of which will contribute value to the organization and the person you are trying to influence.

Outcome #1: Action

One of the most important outcomes that can come from coaching is a profound action-orientation in others. Coaching is a way to light a fire within the other person—and ourselves. When using the Coaching TIPS²™ Model, you spark initiative and create changes in behavior, processes, commitment, and levels of engagement with the work, the team, the customers, and the organization. More importantly, you instill an increased level of empowerment in the coachee to make these changes and the ownership for making them. *We believe that you have to ask yourself, "Is the coachee genuinely engaged in the mission of the organization?" and "Is he or she encouraged, inspired, and determined to make a difference through positive change as a result of this coaching experience?"*

Some coaching conversations can be difficult to have for both coach and coachee, and fear, conflict, and disappointment are just a few of the emotions that may be associated with a given conversation. While these emotions are likely to arise from time to time, the overall goal of a coaching experience is to leave people with hope, confidence, and reassurance about the future.

> *"Many of our fears are tissue-paper-thin, and a single courageous step would carry us clear through them."*
> —Brendan Francis

While not every encounter will be entirely positive, you want the person being coached to be optimistic about the future, despite the unknowns and the very real possibility of failure. Coaches look at failures as learning points, not ending points, and they try to encourage their coachees to look at them in the same way. It isn't the coach's job to stamp out a person's worries; rather, the coach should bring these concerns to light, help put the risks and personal reservations into perspective, and communicate a willingness to provide Support along the way. And while the coachee's uncertainty may never go away completely, showing your confidence in the person and the Plan may instill the needed courage for the coachee to take that first step.

Outcome #2: New Perspectives

The next outcome that the coach should reach for is helping the other person discover new insights and ways of thinking about how they are perceiving their performance and contribution to the organization. Coaching should be an enlightening experience for all parties. If the lines of communication are open enough, and if both coaching partners are willing to drop their preconceived notions and consider the situation from a fresh perspective, you can expect that both parties will experience breakthroughs in their thinking. If the coaching session is effective, you should be able to answer "Yes!" to the following questions:

- *"Is the other person more aware of his or her personal 'blind spots' or opportunities for growth?"*
- *"Do both of us feel that we have new information and a better understanding of the situation and our potential solutions?"*
- *"Does the other person receive positive coaching and reinforcement when their performance is on target?"*

Outcome #3: Candor

The next outcome to strive for is increased candor and honesty. Over the years, we too have been on the receiving end of the coaching process. At one point, one of our coaches told us, *"You can always count on me to tell you the truth as I perceive it."* Since then, it has been apparent to us just how valuable candor and honesty are in terms of helping us maximize our potential and be the best we can be.

While it can be difficult to be so direct, the coach should strive to avoid any ambiguity when discussing the specific focus and purpose of the coaching with the coachee. If people walk away from a conversation lacking a clear understanding of your point of view or the specific feedback you've shared with them, you have missed the core of the coaching process. If your intentions are good and your conversations are candid, not only will people value your opinion, they will trust you to be honest and straightforward with them in the future. However, honest dialogue must go both ways. The coach needs to be candid, but the coachees also need to be given the opportunity to share their honest viewpoints and feelings. To ensure that your message was clear and received as intended, you must ask yourself these two questions:

- *"Did I express my message clearly and provide a specific description of the need, opportunity, or issue I've observed or the strength I'd like to reinforce?"*
- *"Did the coachee seem to appreciate my honesty and respond with candor in return?"*

Outcome #4: Personal Growth

Coaching is most effective when both parties have a sense of being personally challenged by the experience. Organizations must find ways to continually adapt and improve to remain competitive and relevant. Individuals must also continuously improve in order to remain valuable to (and improve the value of) the organization. Coaching pushes people to strive for the next level of learning, performance, and competency. What this means is that sometimes, the coach has to set aside any reservations and boldly ask the coachee to change a little or give a little more when needed. We tell the coachees we work with that the internal rate of change has to exceed the external rate of change. If it doesn't, the organization is on the path to becoming extinct.

Sometimes people sell themselves short but have more to give. A great coach will challenge the tendency to become complacent, instill a sense of possibility, and ask the coachee for a new or greater contribution. The questions the coach should ask are:

- *"Is this person aware that I am asking for and expecting something more?"*
- *"Do they understand that the expectations we have of them have changed?"*
- *"Do they understand that they have to lead their own transformation?"*

Outcome #5: Creativity and Innovation

When two or more minds work together, you have greater capacity to become an innovative force. The synergy or creativity that flows naturally from a coaching conversation can fuel new and bold solutions and spawn fresh action. If you fail to react to (or outright ignore) the creative juices that come bubbling out of a good coaching conversation, you will miss a golden opportunity to create distinctive value. Innovation comes from exploring outside of the box and being willing to take some smart risks. Pushing the boundaries may not always come naturally, so you might need to actively challenge the traditional ways of thinking. When people are open to creative possibilities, they are more likely to discover better practices and more-efficient uses for their time and resources that will produce benefits for the team, organization, customers, and individuals.

In combination, these coaching outcomes will translate into a competitive advantage for the organization. But what these outcomes also create is a passion within all members of the organization to coach others and be coached in order to excel at their work—something we like to call a "coaching culture." Organizations need strong contributors at all levels to achieve better financial performance, grow as a business, and survive and thrive long term. These advantages for the organization also lead to exciting, secure, rewarding, and interesting career opportunities for its members—and all of this happens because coaches have the courage to engage people and actively talk about their professional performance and development. We are all human, and every one of us has some blind spots. But with the help of a coach, we can more easily discover our vulnerabilities and opportunities for improvement, as well as our strengths that need to be reinforced, leveraged, and celebrated. With that understanding, each person will become a valuable asset to the organization. Through coaching, and the use of the Coaching TIPS²™ Model, you have the ability to empower people, unleash discretionary performance in others, and achieve true greatness as an organization.

10

Coaching: A Way of Leading

When things are going well and reinforcement is needed, when there are problems to address, or when opportunities for growth and development exist, coaching is always a good place to start. Creating coaching moments and experiences helps you build a foundation of respect and trust, create a spirit of openness, and improve clarity and understanding so the journey to enhanced performance and learning can begin.

We are confident that you will find coaching to be a whole-life skill that gets results on the job, off the job, and with all types of people: customers, suppliers, stakeholders—anyone with whom you need to build a partnership. Coaching is more than how you talk to people; it's a way of leading others and an intrinsic part of achieving all goals, strategies and targets. It becomes a core part of a leader's value system, something that is fundamental to the way a leader thinks and acts. You can see it in the ways that leaders make themselves available to people, take an authentic interest in their team members and their projects, and recognize and acknowledge the achievements of others; you can also see it in their efforts to collaborate with and genuinely engage others. Coaching reflects who you are and how you operate as a leader in a broader context.

The Coaching TIPS²™ Model in Action

We like to forewarn users of the Coaching TIPS²™ Model that many people may never have experienced a high-quality, relationship-focused coaching session, so this approach to the coaching process may initially feel a little different to your coachees. You may find that at first, your coaching partners won't know how to react to this collaborative coaching approach; they may wonder what your motives are. To combat this, we recommend that you share your intentions and explain your approach ahead of time. Tell people that you are striving to improve your skills as a coach and to build a coaching culture on your team and throughout the organization. You can even explain the philosophy and techniques of the Coaching TIPS²™ Model to the people you are working with so they know what to expect and can support you and even hold you accountable for applying your new skills. Additionally, if your coaching partners know what you are working towards, the feedback they give you will be all the more relevant and helpful. Disclosing your new approach not only helps people see that you too are willing to engage in personal growth and development, but also allows them to understand what they can expect from you.

The importance of doing this in advance became very clear to us when we were coaching Carlos, the plant manager of a large production facility. This hard-nosed, results-driven manager knew that he needed to change his leadership style and adopt a coaching approach. He had risen through the ranks in a difficult working environment and had not had the opportunity to develop the skills needed to be a people-leader. The senior-team environment was very toxic, and it was having an impact on results. When we started working with Carlos, we taught him the Coaching TIPS²™ process and were impressed by his commitment to use the Model with the leadership team that reported to him. Never have we seen a leader try *so hard* to use the Model. That said, we were surprised by the reactions he got from his team members: while some immediately recognized it as an effort to build productive and collaborative relationships, others were completely taken aback by the dramatic and abrupt change in Carlos' demeanor and approach to engaging them. Because they had no idea that he was making conscious changes to his way of interacting and communicating, they interpreted the change as being inauthentic, out of character—and likely to be short-lived. The coaching discussions he had with the senior team were met with skepticism and reluctance. Until Carlos disclosed to his team members what he was trying to accomplish, he didn't get as much traction with his coaching efforts as he would have liked. The lesson is this: coaching will come more easily, and people will be more collaborative, if you are willing to be transparent about your commitment to putting coaching into action.

As you begin to make changes to your coaching, communication, and/or leadership style, it is essential that you remember how important it is to be coachable. Invite people to give you feedback, and model how to accept others' feedback graciously. Make sure they understand that you are always working to amplify your strengths and close the gap on your own opportunities for improvement. The more that you talk openly about the coaching process, the more familiar it will feel to your team members and the more accepting of it they will be. To further instill coaching as part of your organization's culture, encourage all members of your team to learn and use coaching skills themselves. Whether we recognize it or not, all members of a group influence one another. Promoting a positive and supportive coaching approach will further enhance the performance of the entire team.

When it comes right down to it, coaching is a common-sense skill needed in all kinds of organizations. As you can see, the Coaching TIPS² ™ Model, derived from years of research and work with managers at all levels, is simply a set of "how-to" skills that leaders, and all willing individual contributors, can learn and use to perform the coaching task more effectively. Remember, you don't have to use all of the tips in the Model each time you coach or try to influence someone. The Coaching TIPS² ™ Model is a template for a discussion, not a set script, and each coaching conversation will have its own unique rhythm. When you begin the discussion, avoid being rigid with your talking points or developing a predictable routine. Let your instincts and inspiration guide you through these conversations and simply use each tip of the Model to guide the message you wish to send.

When coaching, and especially when you encounter coaching opportunities on the fly, keep your message short and simple without being abrupt. If you can limit the conversation to the most important "takeaways" for the other person, the coaching session will be more concise and less confusing. That said, you can't count on every conversation to be brief, and you may need to develop patience during conversations that consume more time. The goal is to make sure that all of the coaching conversations you have are productive, regardless of their length. Learn to trust the Coaching TIPS²™ Model to pull you through.

In some ways, using the Model it is a little bit like attempting to land an airplane on a foggy day: the pilot has to trust the on-board instruments because the target or landing area isn't always visible from the air. In coaching, you can't always predict where you're going to end up. Sometimes you and the coachee will need to feel your way through the Topic and Impact as you prepare to find the best solution. If you deftly navigate through the TIPS²™ methods and skills and communicate your thoughts clearly, the coaching process will very naturally take you where you need to go. But remember, this is not a linear process. It is dynamic and there is no "paint by numbers" formula to follow when you get into the thick of it. Diligently following the Coaching TIPS²™ Model does not guarantee your success, even if your communication is crystal clear. Some interactions will be difficult, and some topics will be more complex, challenging, and contentious than others. Stay optimistic during these times and don't bury your head in the sand when things aren't going your way. Change often happens gradually, and we believe that coaching is an ongoing process that consists of some art and some science. You'll need to use your judgment to decide how to approach the timing, message, length, and intensity of the conversation, as well as when to revisit the coaching topic at another time.

As a coach, it is always better to be proactive and strategic rather than reactionary, but please don't assume this means that strategic, future-focused coaching is the only situation in which coaching will be necessary. On the contrary, half or more of all the coaching conversations you will have will result from you noticing, observing, or seeing a coaching opportunity after the fact—and nowhere is this truer than in a virtual setting.

Using the Coaching TIPS²™ Model in a Virtual Setting

Virtual coaching—coaching for those who work and lead from a distance—can be accomplished very successfully by using the Coaching TIPS²™ Model. Early research in this area shows that distance coaching can be just as effective as when it's done face-to-face. However, the challenges of virtual coaching are more apparent when video conferencing is not possible. In that situation, the body language and vocal cues that we depend on to help us send and receive accurate messages are missing, so communicating accurately is more difficult—especially given the ever-changing array of communication technologies that have tried to take their place, often unsuccessfully. This leaves plenty of room for misunderstandings. To make up for the missing non-verbal communication cues, we recommend that you conduct your coaching conversations by phone whenever possible. Voice communication helps to reduce misunderstandings because all parties on the call can hear the emotions of others, pauses in the conversation, and vocal intonations. When speaking on the phone, be extra careful to listen actively and convey your thoughts in a clear, concise way. When you have finished, ask the other person to summarize what you've said to ensure that the message you intended to send is the one that was received:

- *"I've really enjoyed talking with you today. Thanks for taking the time to discuss your plan for this assignment. Let's review what we've covered so we are both clear... Does that sound right to you?"*

Since you can't see or decipher non-verbal communication cues during phone calls, ask open-ended questions to make up the shortfall:

- *How does this make you feel?*
- *What are your initial reactions?*
- *Do you believe this is a good idea?*

Pay special attention to the person's voice (tone, volume, rate of speech, pauses) to help you detect additional information (i.e., any excitement, nervousness, frustration, etc. that the person may be experiencing). You may also consider closing your eyes while speaking on the phone. This helps to block out the distractions around you so you can more easily pick up on auditory cues. Avoid using the "speaker" feature on your phone whenever possible. Using this function can suggest to the other person that you are multitasking, and that being able to do other things while you're on the phone is more important to you than ensuring that your voice is clear and easily understood. Aside from video conferencing, coaching phone calls seem to be to best possible method for conducting initial or formal coaching conversations. However, when following up on an initial coaching discussion, we do recommend using less-formal methods, such as text messages, instant messages, and email.

Some Closing Thoughts on Coaching

When we introduce the Coaching TIPS²™ Model to people in workshops or when doing executive coaching, we always encourage them to begin using the concepts and skills as soon as they can, and to start with a coaching situation where achieving a successful outcome is highly probable. At the same time, we implore people not to wait for the "ideal" coaching situation—one may never be found, and they are all so different! We also try to remind people to be patient; no one can expect to see dramatic results overnight. As with every new skill, developing competence in this area will take time, practice, the right mentality, trust in yourself, and a lot of persistence.

Speaking about the importance of having a high level of personal persistence and mental and physical endurance reminds us of the story of Cliff Young, an unassuming individual who competed in a high-endurance race. As it turned out, the race he decided to compete in is one of the world's most challenging ultra-marathons: the 543.7-mile endurance race from Sydney to Melbourne, Australia. In 1983, 61-year-old Cliff Young showed up to the race wearing overalls and work boots and picked up his race number alongside a group of world-class athletes. Immediately, people doubted his ability to finish the race. In response, he said, *"Yes I can. See, I grew up on a farm where we couldn't afford horses or tractors, and the whole time I was growing up, whenever the storms would roll in, I'd have to go out and round up the sheep. We had 2,000 sheep on 2,000 acres. Sometimes I would have to run those sheep for two or three days. It took a long time, but I'd always catch them. I believe I can run this race."* As expected, on the first day of the race, Cliff quickly fell behind the other runners due to his odd approach to running; people described it as a "shuffle." This race typically took about five days to complete, which required the athletes to run for about 18 hours and then sleep for six. Cliff wasn't aware of this conventional race strategy and, much to the surprise of the spectators and other runners, he had the endurance needed to continue on without sleeping. As each night passed, he got closer and closer to being in the lead—and he just stayed consistent and kept going. By the final night, Cliff Young crossed the finish line, and not only did he cross it first, but he also set a new course record. His approach is now referred to as the "Young-Shuffle" by ultra-marathoners and is considered to be more energy-efficient than other approaches. Being a world-class coach also takes some stamina and consistent effort. It is something that has to be sustained over time. Don't let your success as a coach be short-lived. Make a commitment today to find the endurance you need to be a coach who will positively impact the people around you and drive the results you seek. Will you trip and fall? Yes. Will the road be steep or uneven at times? Definitely. Don't doubt your ability to develop this important skill set. Keep shuffling along towards that end goal.

The result we want for you is to create a true coaching culture in your organization and help others feel empowered by your use of the Coaching TIPS2™ Model. We want your people to *want* to seek out your coaching input and expertise in the future. We want to help you create a working environment where people feel comfortable sharing their concerns, opportunities, and problems and gaining the most from accomplishments. We want you to leave a lasting leadership legacy through your efforts to influence and guide others in their personal-development journeys.

"I never cease to be amazed at the power of the coaching process to draw out the skills or talent that was previously hidden within an individual, and which invariably finds a way to solve a problem previously thought unsolvable."

—John Russell, Former Managing Director, Harley Davidson Europe Ltd.

APPENDIX

The Coaching TIPS²™ Workshop from CMOE

About the Workshop

CMOE's Coaching TIPS²™ Workshop is designed to help participants develop practical and effective coaching skills that can be applied when influencing others, working through obstacles, and achieving results through others. The workshop is based on CMOE's Coaching TIPS²™ Model—a proven process that is backed by extensive and ongoing research. The Model is a flexible and dynamic communication road map that leaders use to interact more effectively in a coaching situation. In the workshop, participants learn how to

- Maximize team-member performance and results through coaching.
- Resolve differences and handle obstacles or resistance.
- Help people adjust to and acquire ownership for changes in the organization.
- Maximize the potential of team members by engaging in developmental coaching discussions.
- Build positive and supportive relationships with team members.
- Achieve bottom-line results while being less controlling.
- Build a coaching culture.

Learning Methods

All of CMOE's workshops are offered in a variety of delivery formats, including live classroom, virtual classroom, or web-based classrooms. The length of the course is flexible and depends largely on the delivery method chosen.

Experienced CMOE facilitators lead workshops from any location of your choosing. We also offer a Train-the-Trainer service in which we provide the skills and knowledge necessary to teach your in-house facilitator or facilitation team how to deliver any CMOE workshop at any time. Clients who choose this option simply purchase the participant materials from CMOE on an as-needed basis once they are certified to teach the program.

Customization

One of CMOE's strongest capabilities is developing customized solutions to meet each organization's unique needs. Contact us for help deciding which level will fulfill the needs of your organization best. You can learn more about CMOE's Coaching TIPS² and Coaching Skills Workshops and how they will benefit your organization by calling us at +1 801 569 3444, filling out an inquiry form on our website (www.CMOE.com), or sending an e-mail to info@cmoe.com.

Other Titles by CMOE Press

- *Candor: How to Have Courageous Coaching Conversations When It Really Matters*

- *The Team Approach: With Teamwork Anything is Possible*

- *Leading Groups to Solutions: A Practical Guide for Facilitators and Team Members*

- *Ahead of the Curve: A Guide to Applied Strategic Thinking*

- *Strategy is Everyone's Job: A Guide to Strategic Leadership*

- *Teamwork: We Have Met the Enemy and They are Us*

- *The Coach: Creating Partnerships for a Competitive Edge*

- *Win-Win Partnerships: Be on the Leading Edge with Synergistic Coaching*

You can purchase the titles above by calling +1 801 569 3444, visiting us online at www.CMOE.com, or ordering them from www.amazon.com.

Connect and Continue the Journey

Visit and Comment on CMOE's Blog
http://www.cmoe.com/blog

Connect with CMOE on LinkedIn
http://www.linkedin.com/company/cmoe

Connect with CMOE on Google+
http://goo.gl/BZNmX